John Byrne Leicester Warren

Searching the Net

A Book of Verses

John Byrne Leicester Warren

Searching the Net

A Book of Verses

ISBN/EAN: 9783337168100

Printed in Europe, USA, Canada, Australia, Japan

Cover: Foto ©Thomas Meinert / pixelio.de

More available books at **www.hansebooks.com**

SEARCHING THE NET

A Book of Verses

By JOHN LEICESTER WARREN
AUTHOR OF 'PHILOCTETES'

"Searching the net of sense which binds us in."
Old Play

CONTENTS.

THE DEFEAT OF GLORY

THE BIRD OF MY LOVE

A MIDDLE-CLASS TRAGEDY

LOVE SHADOWS

AN OCEAN GRAVE

OPHELIA

SIGH HEART, BREAK NOT

SEPARATED FORTUNES

A RENUNCIATION

THE REDBREAST

RETROSPECT

AN AUTUMN SERENADE

A FAREWELL

CONTENTS.

	PAGE.
THE CARDINAL'S LAMENT	76
MEDEA	92
NATURE'S RENEWING	109
JAEL	112
A SKETCH AT EVENING	128
NEMESIS	130
RURAL EVENING	137
ONE VIEW OF WORSHIP	141
A MEETING AND ADVICE	147
THE TWO OLD KINGS	152
ARROW OF LOVE	166
ODE TO THE SUN	172
A MADRIGAL	182
THE GARDEN OF DELIGHT	187
IN SICILY	190
THE SHEPHERD AND THE HIRELING	196
AT THE COUNCIL	199

THE DEFEAT OF GLORY.

Porphyry beams dull-rosy in their light,
    With architraves of alabaster cold,
And column-heads expanding into slight
    Long arabesques of intertwisting gold;

Along the ceiling runs the giant war,
    And Jove in lurid halo; all his hand,
Poising to hurl Enceladus afar,
    Red with the ruin of the Titan band.

So stately is the chamber, where a King,
    Feeble, in dim eclipse of human power,
Lies, with dull orbs or slowly widening
    Eyelids, to stare away the vacant hour.

The couch of death is glorious where he lies ;
   Its silver canopies forbid the rays.
Sun, shine not on his pillow till he dies,—
   Time's tyrant once, and emperor of days !

Though all his precinct glitter to its roof,
   Tho' regal the surroundings of his end,
No palace-floors are ever phantom-proof
   When shadows of a greater King ascend.

The pale hours of the dawning at his bed
   Bend each in turn to pity him and pass,
Who drave his hook in nations. Now, instead,
   Moans are the only edicts that he has.

Alone some weary sighing in his rest
   Invades the calmness of his face asleep—
So, when day's beacon embers in red west,
   An awful rumour heaves the wailing deep.

THE DEFEAT OF GLORY.

Sleep, broken thing of glory, wreck of kings,
    A dubious sleep of waning pulses bred ;
Sleep, as thou art, a scorn to living things,
    Derision to the dumb and patient dead !

Once at thy feet great princes crawled in mire,
    Thy face for wonderment and worship was
To these as Phœbus, helmed with early fire,
    Raying his intervals of ocean-glass.

O faded eyes untouched with royal light,
    Lean lips without desire of wine or bread ;
O silent features folded with the night
    Wherein is no man's deed remembered.

Thy gold is changed to dross, thy rose to weed ;
    Thy raiment is the grave's sepulchral sheet,
They push thee where no lute shall praise thy deed,
    They fold thy yellow hands and parchment feet.

In silk and silver blue thy reign begins,
   Thine end is sore; and surely stricken worse,
Than that goat limping to the sea of sins,
   Sick with the burthen of a nation's curse.

If one keen ray thy lattice enters round,
   Thy loathing eyeballs ache, are troubled, weep.
Thou groanest, tho' no man hath given thee wound,
   And thou art drowsy yet for all thy sleep.

The orange urns around thy colonnade,
   With heavy odour call the rover bee.
But thou art ague-broken, and afraid
   Where no fear is; what are such things to thee?

Thine ears retain no murmur from the street;
   To thee dim rain is one with earnest noon;
Thy dull brain cannot catch the perfume sweet,
   When the field deepens into perfect June.

THE DEFEAT OF GLORY.

The record of thy days becomes a blot;
    The yearling infant calls its sister's name.
O princely phantom, with thy fame forgot,
    Move, if thou canst, thy lips and do the same.

Thy white hands only tremble on the sheet,
    Tho' thy Prætorian legions watch around,
And under echoing archways in the heat
    The feet of many sentinels resound.

All night the melancholy bugle calls,
    All hours goes on the guardian soldier's pace.
Arms clash at dawn within the warrior halls,
    And drums in thunder wake the market-place.

And chamberlains in muffled anteroom
    Enter on velvet insteps, "Will he last?"
The whisper goes, "Another week of gloom,
    Must our horizon still be overcast?"

"Must this old darkness yet in heaven remain?
　New orb of gold ascend, the time is weak;
Thy sweet young ray is ready and we are fain;
　On radiant feet these chaining vapours break!"

"Shall this unworthy remnant of a throne
　Perplex our statists with his lingering breath?
Shall his heirs wait nor dare to clutch their own,
　Watching a sire's most tedious feud with death?"

"Shall he entombed be emperor of them,
　Shall this dust threaten and these bones command?
Must his hoar brows usurp a diadem,
　Shall he play tyrant with a palsied hand?"

So runs upon their lips thine epitaph;
　The men whom thou hast benched and warmed
　　　with meat,
These utter abjects hear thy name and laugh,
　Mere river-flies hatched in thine empire's heat.

THE DEFEAT OF GLORY.

And this disdain is fallen to thy last days,—
   Who wast alone for glory, with thy throne
Built as a rock in sides of pleasant ways—
   That all men tire of thee and wish thee gone.

Therefore, I hold the dead are more than kings :
   They are not cold or hungry or dismayed.
They dwell together where no morning springs,
   They waken to no toil, and are not paid

At even-tide with wage. No maiden's word
   Hath given them mirth. At no lord's yoke they
      weep.
The song of love their silence never heard,
   Their feet are tangled in deep nets of sleep.

God hath discarded them as broken things ;
   They shall not hear, descending from his throne,
Some angel with great amber sweep of wings.
   He hath chidden them out as abjects from his own.

Yea, earth is weary that they were at all,
    And heaven remembers not that they have been.
The pale grass hangs above them like a wall.
    Dim is their chamber and their hall unseen.

Therefore, old king, thy bed shall be seven-fold
    More bitter, strewn with theirs; because thou must
For all thy beaming gates and treasure-hold
    Gain at God's hand some inches of red dust.

Yea, as dry boughs of some dismembered tree,
    Numb from thy nape to thy heels buskin-shod,
Thy shrouded limbs and side-bound hands shall be
    Crushed down in darkness from the face of God.

Yea, that white fluttered seraph-choir of his
    Hate thy lean bones as terrors; ay, they dread
To unbind the banded jaws, and eye-places
    Where the balls wither inward at the head.

And, ere this come, such toil of heavy breath
    By this old royal phantom runs to worse
Than yon gaunt image of sepulchral death;
    Life is a garment burning like a curse,

When weary pulses flicker in disease,
    And Pain draws tortured Reason from its seat;
To anguish and an age of maladies
    Is not the grave a rest supremely sweet?

Better to sleep in barrows, where young lambs
    Feed and repose in daisies o'er the dead,
Where, moving with a chime of necks, their dams
    Graze round the belfry silent overhead.

Where in among the fleeces of the sheep,
    Like small and burnished rooks, the starlings call,
Between black crosses in the field of sleep,
    And make the mild spring weather musical.

Leave this bright dream; return, with bated breath
   Enter the shrouded palace where he dies;
Say, can the splendid precinct of his death
   Like one field daisy soothe thine aching eyes,

Sick with all human artifice of gold?
   The need of nature deepens in a breast
That, having laid its dead in hallowed mould,
   Loathing at fame, finds nature comfort best.

All things are doomed and alter from their birth.
   Man sighs at eve who rose at morn to sing.
Gaze on this couch, and answer; is it worth
   A loaf, a leaf, one feather to be king?

O'er thee sour Æsculapian vultures stoop,
   And heirs with greedy eyes peruse thy bed;
And itching fingers feel each signet hoop,
   And eager chins examine, " Is he dead?"

THE DEFEAT OF GLORY.

He is not dead, if one lean lifted hand
    Redeem him from thy nations, king of sleep—
As some brown sea-weed on the margin strand,
    Torn from the inmost gardens of the deep,

Attains with earthly flowers no root or rest,
    But lies and festers among sand and surge;
The burnished breakers hither heave and crest,
    There haggard darnels taste the east wind's scourge.

Life in blue armour, crowned with ardent hair,
    Hath scorned this outworn wreck of human breath,
And flung him out beyond her temple stair
    To wait the rising of the floods of death.

He is dying out, tho' under stately fanes,
    The arch-priest wrestles for his monarch still
In organ-litanies; he is faint and wanes;
    He is meaner than the lizard on the hill,

Who sniffs the early air with lithe grey throat,
    Whose wild eyes taste the increase of the morn ;
Who sees her olive interspaces float,
    In rims of ardent amber newly born.

God folds away his night and calls the red ;
    The creeping thing hath pleasure in his deed.
In these dim eyes where reason's light is dead,
    The rose-bud is one colour with the reed.

As some old branch neglects its foliage lost,
    The hand of him forgets its early power.
As some grey garden-plot in utter frost,
    Whence all is starved, except a bitter flower,

Which lingers in mid-winter's extreme cold,
    When wholesome herbs are perished long ago.
So lives his lettered name, in imaged gold
    His picture, his long titles in a row.

Mock him with sounding pomp no more. In vain
    Number to him no nations, where he is
By name as God incarnate. Ah, refrain
    The irony of bending knees to *this!*

The weary sunbeams crawl themselves away.
    The walls are laned with shadow in the moon.
He is almost gone, each turn of night and day,
    He wanes from swoon to sleep, from dream to swoon;

As scribes are busy in great parchment scrolls
    To set his acts and annals chronicled;
And paint large letters all along the rolls,
    Gold for his glory, for his warfare red.

They count the array of chariots, as he fought,
    His wives, his tankards curious at carouse;
His captives, the wrought lions of his court,
    His archers; all the increase of his house,

His chests of sewn work, armour arrow-proof,
  His dædal girdles, and unwoven bales
Of crisp wool ready for his hand-maid's woof,
  His hammered bowls, their topaz-headed nails;

The woven strewings of his mirrored floors,
  The keen root-dust, that, mingled in his wines,
Arose an incense over corridors
  To ceilings made as heaven with twelve great signs.

And it ran in their writing, how the vines
  Seemed ripened in the favour of his word.
He had goodly horse to lead in battle-lines,
  Upon all nations he unsheathed one sword.

And bound his net on their imperious head,
  And wound around them evil as a toil;
And laid their rugged lips of laughter dead,
  And meted out their empire into spoil.

To the firm west he flung a blast of war,
    On the light east he strengthened his array;
" All men are foes, who yet unconquered are,
    My faulchion holds a rebel world at bay,"

He cried, almighty in his silver hall;
    Peace knew his smile, his frown concluded death.
At his approach the watch-tower on the wall
    Trembled, the rampart melted at his breath.

Into the sun-death raught his empire bounds;
    Far to his foot-stool from the dawning place
Came orient kings to watch his eyes, as hounds,
    Who whimper chidden before a master's face.

In virgin waves his mariners held oars,
    His merchants traded in secluded fairs.
Strange Triton gods beheld thro' temple doors
    His sails, as floated sea-birds, unawares.

His multitude of rowing sailors sate
  Strong-handed in their benches. The black deep
In bitter furrows hoarse against them. Fate
  Ready to whelm them in each water-heap.

Yet in the teeth of death with wrist and arm
  They pushed a passage on. The blind wind died
Vexed at their masterdom. The surf ran calm,
  Or washed faint edges on the galley's side.

Till, where the hungry deep wrought yesterday,
  Are laid its morsels, violet water-shells,
And starry orange creatures of the spray,
  And leathery bladder-weeds with egg-like cells;

And washed mosaics out of wave-worn floors,
  And limpet shells unanchored from rock root,
With small dried rearing horse-heads, on the shores,
  By prickly balls of sea, like chestnut fruit;

And drifts of nether ocean rough in thorn—
    All sea-wrack wafted harvest; lord, for thee
The villagers gleaned coral-branches torn
    In far deeps from the rosy mother tree.

And red-grey fisher-cities, terraced in
    With bushes on some broken headland's face,
Drew down each dawn their grating keels to win
    The shell reserved for princes and their race.

So thou didst bathe thy mantle in its dyes;
    The bearded murex for thy purple bled:
Thou satest sanguine as the sunset skies,
    With bands of burning jewels on thy head;

So some were almost slain to gaze on thee,
    In thy full royalty and glory seat;
Strong men, in spirit melting utterly,
    Beheld with failing knees and feeble feet.

All sea-deeps to thy pilots lay revealed,
 As to a husbandman; who, spring and fall,
Has ploughed and sown one sour unyielding field,
 Noting each nook and corner of it all.

They learnt the secret teeth of every shoal,
 The reef-guards round each treasure isle of main,
Whose mountain sides the miner like a mole
 Enters to dig the beryl in his vein.

They sought sweet calamus in reedy wands,
 And capes with spice-trees under their ravines;
And orchard havens up in austere lands
 To bring strange berries to delight thy queens.

Or thy slow mules toiled down some mountain stair
 Where all the cliffs are broken, and with shocks
The ice-wind flaps the barren steep, in bare
 Heaven and the lonely fields of tumbled rocks.

THE DEFEAT OF GLORY.

Strange oil they brought thee from no olive tree;
   Where float the frozen islands thou didst man
Thy boats to row Cimmerian glooms of sea
   And fling the barb against leviathan.

And from secluded gardens of the east,
   They found thee singing children, blue at eyes,
Bright as the rain is, beautiful; the least
   Among them worth a city's ransom price.

They bought sleek girls with silver to thy will,
   And thou didst take thy joy with each of these.
Their voices were as some low chiming rill,
   Their stature as a hedge of almond-trees.

So like a moon thy soul shone lifted up,
   By reason of thy dainties, and it said.
"The incense of a world perfumes my cup,
   The wheat of empires ambers for my bread.

"God hath set morning lights for me in heaven
    To quicken my uprising; he unbinds
The sweet rain in my homage : mine the seven
    Great northern stars, mine the four region winds.

"I yoke all nations on my wagon wheel;
    All fruit of earth is mine; all bales as well
The strong ships carry; all thou dost conceal
    Their gray gigantic sea unsearchable.

"All toil and increase to my feet are brought;
    My palace is a cage, where each delight
Dwells; as a bright bird hunted down and caught
    To sleek her pretty feathers in my sight.

"All spirits, bond and free, are mine to use;
    I make all seasons sweet to my desire.
And when the hard frost lies, where lay soft dews,
    In every winter-house a cedar fire

"Lends gracious heat: you would not guess the year
    That pushes icy shoulders at the doors
Of poor men's huts. A land of bloom is here
    Weaving an ample summer on my floors.

"Against the ruddy lamp of my renown,
    As some great Pharos light in stormy heaven,
The lesser princedoms shatter wildly blown,
    And rend their helmless realms, as foam is riven.

"I am set for God, to rivet or unwind,
    To establish or remove at my decree.
I alter and abolish, break or bind;
    Shall any power perplex my deity?

"I am for ever; no decay makes wan
    The eternal crown that gleams against my brow
Death is my bondsman, Pain my wage-woman,
    Age is at league with me." Behold thee now!

THE BIRD OF MY LOVE.

Thou wilt not hearken, though I weep
    Hot tears against thy folded hands;
Though Love, this exile bird we keep,
    Sits pining for his radiant lands;
Sick of some tiny fleck or mote,
He never sings us now a single note.

He hangs his head, his eyelids close,
    The gloss is faded on his wing;
So broken down he seems with woes,
    He may not pipe us anything.
I call; his pale lips quiver loth;
Is then his song all over for us both?

THE BIRD OF MY LOVE.

Thy captive, his were early chains,
    The noose was laid of woven hairs;
Thy tame bird, he would count the grains
    Thy pity gave him unawares.
He was bound in with golden bars,
Till he forgot the weather and the stars.

All day he saw thee near his cage;
    To watch thee, moving or in rest,
Became the poor bird's only wage;
    When thy hand fed him he was best.
He gave thee every note and trill,
And piped his little welcome with a will.

And so he sang till yesterday,—
    Came to the bars with many a bend;
His music made the old soft way,
    Till sleep fell on him, and the end.
Laid in his sand now, cold and grey,
    Interpret me his latest honey-lay.

I think he sang, " I am only thine,
   I am broken if thou leavest me ;
I faint if thou art gone, divine ;
   This is no prison if near thee.
My heart floods out to thee in song,
And in thy smile my melody is strong.

" Take freedom, God's own gift on all,—
   Remove Heaven's joy, and leave me none ;
Take light, life's highest festival,
   And leave me blind beneath the sun
To do thy bidding, sweet, all day,
Take all except thy dearest self away."

We kept him caged, and he is dead.
   We did unwisely, doing so ;
Between his prison wires was shed
   A meadow breath, which laid him low.
He loved thee much, but pined unseen,
And brake his heart when woods grew tender green.

THE BIRD OF MY LOVE.

Love is thy cage-bird, like to die;
   He mopes, is weary, must begone;
He finds no favour in thine eye,
   Or answer in thine altered tone.
Thy god will pine as pined the bird,—
Each gave free heaven away for thy sweet word.

O changeful queen of many wiles,
   Why lure and tend me for a whim,
And waste thy hundred pretty smiles
   A season, till the love grows dim
Between thy rose lips unawares?
Fickle, they change. Unaltered I am theirs.

Doth all love end in weariness?
   The music falters in his string;
The arms grow faint in their caress,
   Which bound me like a marriage ring.
What have I failed in then, my sweet,
That I must weep for pity at thy feet?

At light offence Love opens wing,
    For sorry reason he will go ;
At straws, which casual breezes fling
    Against his feet, his angers glow.
In all my thought I cannot touch
One crime, save loving thee, my love, too much.

Bid me begone, but tell me why,
    That I may mend what is amiss.
Love, I am patient ; earnestly
    I will search out and alter this.
Reprove, and I will earn new praise,
Increasing due observance of love's ways.

Thy frown is like a winter house,
    Laid eastward in a bitter land,
Whose roads are full of frozen boughs,
    And rough in ruts of snow and sand ;
In white chains hangs the spider's woof,
Where keen winds freeze in ice-teeth at my roof.

THE BIRD OF MY LOVE.

There heaven is stayed from dew, and dry
    The ice-sheet saws upon the reeds.
The wind is up with a wailing cry,
    The deep has wrought and flung its weeds.
The blotted sun went long ago,
And the stained cliffs are keen in furrowed snow.

I have been weary with such days;
    Let this grey change to rose again.
Indeed, but it shall dim thy praise
    To leave me out in sweeping rain.
My spring waits only thy command,
The seasons of my soul are in thy hand.

The iron day declines. The flower
    Returns in seams of mountain grey;
Fresh leaves adorn the faded bower;
    And Spring, who gave his lute away,
Above blue bands of wintry night
Arises in a fan of blinding light!

A MIDDLE-CLASS TRAGEDY.

Lonely I went by a highway-road track
    Threading a desolate level;
Leafless the hedges, the herbage lay black,
    Fit for swine flocks of the devil.

Nothing less evil such pasture could tread:
    Drosses and dregs of the city
Broad-cast abolished the clover, and spread
    In a vitriol scum without pity.

Here they had flayed the field-faces for brick,
    Here the black sails of great mills
Flapped round in ruins, despondently sick,
    Strident, rehearsing their ills.

Near them a woman sat making her moan,
    Deep in the slow-creeping glooms.
A hedge at her back and her feet on a stone,
    Pale as a tenant of tombs.

I was a penman without coin or birth,
    Chained to a desk with a quill.
"Nobody needs me the least upon earth,
    If I save her some one will.

"Some one I need to expect me at eve,
    Some one to love me of right,
To drudge all the week for, that she may receive
    A pound more on Saturday night.

"A weed! well, no matter: the weed bloom is sweet,
    A stray! who am I to complain?
So only she love me, I'll kneel to her feet,
    Forgetting their highway stain.

"Who without scorn there had passed thee? Not one.
    Faded, O love, was thine eye.
Frozen almost in the rain-blast alone,
    Cherish her, lest she may die."

Past rode a banker, his hat-brim was wide;
    Sleek came a Levite in view,
Crossed at a trot to the opposite side,
    Sniffing his tithe over-due.

Knaves, let them go; their abhorrence is praise,
    Scorning that greatens my prize.
Swine are these, folded with fat round their face;
    Sweet, O my pearl, then arise.

Let me recover this thing on my lips,
    Utterly mine, loved of none.
Let my life cherish her dead finger tips;
    Let my blood make her pulse run.

A MIDDLE-CLASS TRAGEDY.

Live for her only that she may have mirth,
    Derelict, waif of the night;
Birthright I've none like the choice of the earth;
    Delicate things are their right.

Firm in one counsel I builded my nest,
    Mine is she now, that was vile;
Utterly mine, what she was matters least,
    Let the world sneer, I can smile.

Love I had need of, and ever so great
    Will to give love where I chose;
Training my fancy to baffle my fate,
    Perfect she seemed as a rose.

Lovely I held her, tho' faded indeed,
    Queen of all wifedom and love;
On sweet delusion I feasted my need,
    Till my soul freshened and throve.

Till a rich neighbour in mischievous play,
    Satyr and exquisite, chose
Once, like a lurcher, to loiter my way,
    Feeling his track by his nose.

Cried, "Who is she, that this boor of a clerk
    Treasures so close in his nest?
Of all sweet birds flocking in to my ark
    Surely his ring-dove is best.

"Why should he smooth her sleek feathers alone,
    Why this monopoly claim?
Pipe to her, fowler, thy mellowest tone,
    'Tice her, then trample her tame."

So to her ear he trilled poison, till she
    Said, "I am all that he sings;
Coarse is my master, plebeian; but he
    Lovely, begotten of kings.

"Will he not love me in houses of gold?
    Hateful this hovel of clay;
Here I sit penned like a sheep to my fold;
    Shall I mope longer a day?

"New lover noble, my true lover strong,
    Make me thine own till we die.
Let this old scarecrow to whom I belong
    Whistle, his cage-bird will fly.

"There you will wrap me in raiment and wreaths,
    Feed me with beautiful flowers;
Days in this cabin are so many deaths,
    Ashes and fetters my hours.

"Chained to his desk my love, ragged indeed,
    Leans; well he loved me at least.
Look at my lord on his wing-footed steed
    Chasing in crimson the beast.

"Is he not beautiful, utterly fair,
  Carelessly sweet his caress?
Is not my clerk out-at-elbows, threadbare,
  Pinching to buy me a dress?

"Kind enough always, poor indigent soul!
  Ah! but that other, a god,
Leads me, and loves me, and seems to control
  Life with a finger, a nod!

"Grey love, adieu! See, I wave you a hand!
  Drive on in patience your quill:
Life to a bountiful river expand;
  Here it ran cramped to a rill."

So, like a flash, she fled off to his towers,
  Over the river-wood there.
Fed here awhile in his precinct of flowers
  Queen, and immortally fair.

A MIDDLE-CLASS TRAGEDY.

Lo, what befell in his palace of light!
    Love in a week became pain.
Till he cried, "Pack thee out, wench, to the night,
    Rot in the ditch or the drain.

"Why, thou art ugly as Erebus seen
    Near, plain as death to my view;
Wasted thy cheek, and I thought thee a queen,
    The other fool made such ado.

"Push her out hastily, night-chill begins;
    Stifle her petulant breath.
Forth as my scape-goat go freighted with sins:
    Crawl to the waters of death.

"Wise-working Nature ordains me scot-free;
    She for my sin dies; it's well.
She is no firstling of kids sent by me,
    Down salt dry reaches of hell.

"First? no, nor last. 'Tis an excellent game;
   This wise old world *will* have play.
So it transfers to her shoulders the blame
   Out of a nobleman's way.

"World, on sweet hinges, run lightly and smooth,
   Feed us, the poor ones will pay!
Primest of pasturage beckon our tooth!
   Rot, thou jade, till the last day!"

Out she was pushed by a varlet in black:
   Warned it was penal to linger:
Feathers and lace on her head and her back,
   Rings raying fire round her finger.

So, the tale runs, he has ruined my life,
   For a week's pastime, it's clear.
He, a great nobleman, covets my wife,
   Clerk on a hundred a year.

"LOVE SHADOWS."

Soul of love, life's only light,
Near thee, clothed in thy delight,
 The dreaming of one dream of pain
 Hath wakened me unblest.

Ay, and rest is near thee sweet;
But one dream-word will repeat
 Sullen echoes, sad as rain,
 In sorrow on my rest.

And a whisper comes and goes
As mine eyelids vainly close,
 "Time thy darling's cheek will stain,
 Years thy love may test."

"LOVE SHADOWS."

"Love endures not locks of grey.
Time, my lovers, looks your way,
 Angry that ye are so fain,
  He creeps to spoil your nest."

Time is wroth because I steal
Waxen lips for my love's seal;
 That thy kisses are as dew,
  As faint warm gales thy sighs.

Thou art lovely in each word,
With ways gentler than a bird;
 Thy delight is always new
  As hunger or sun-rise.

Time the serpent lies concealed
In the city, by the field;
 We are clay beneath his hand
  To leave and hate our joys.

"LOVE SHADOWS."

Time an adder lurks and glides
In Love's pleasant pasture-sides,
    He hears vows many as the sand,
        Broken soon as toys.

Time and Farewell hand in hand,
As sighing reeds, grey shadows stand
    And whisper, "life is not more dear
        Than this nest they have strown;

"Can he leave her?" Farewell sighs,
"I will rend them tho' each dies;
    One boy's trouble, one maid's tear
        Are nothing; both mine own!

"This girl is pretty as she lies
With the tear half in her eyes;
    And he seems, as if her breath
        Made his own heart go.

"Time my brother, Death my friend,
Each relent; I never bend;
    Tho' I seem less hard than Death,
      I am utter steel and snow.

"I bring fair faces to grey dust,
I change to loathing maiden trust,
    As pear-bloom crumbles under rain;
      I, Farewell, can do this.

"For Love I bargain; he is sold.
I alter sweet lips into cold.
    I rend as Death does, and my pain
      Is terrible as his.

"I let live but I can teach
Two souls, aching each for each,
    To live and never meet again,
      To love and never kiss."

"LOVE SHADOWS."

So the shadow seemed to say,
And melted on the morning ray,
    And I turned, and found my Pearl
    Sweeter for surprise.

Night is long and dreams are fleet ;
I will deem their visions, sweet,
    Light as that least ripple curl,
    That on thy temple lies.

Hold in mine thy rose lips fast ;
Who shall say which kisses last ?
    What, tho' weeping-ripe, my girl,
    Smile thro' rainy eyes.

Love me ; spring goes ; every hour
Beats out petals from the flower.
    What, dear heart, if love be shed
    Under foot as soon ?

"LOVE SHADOWS."

Shall the rolling month lay mute
Honey word and tender suit?
   Shall the discord of the dead
   Alter all Love's tune?

Ah, we know not; but indeed
It may sweeten true Love's need,
   Hearing near a phantom tread,
   Black in golden noon.

AN OCEAN GRAVE.

My Love lies in the gates of foam,
  The last dear wreck of shore;
The naked sea-marsh binds her home,
  The sand her chamber door.

The grey gulls flap the written stones,
  The ox-birds chase the tide;
And near that narrow field of bones
  Great ships at anchor ride.

Black piers with crust of dripping green,
  One foreland, like a hand,
O'er intervals of grass between
  Grey lonely dunes of sand.

A church of silent weathered looks,
    A breezy reddish tower,
A yard whose mounded resting-nooks
    Are tinged with sorrel flower.

In peace the swallow's eggs are laid
    Along the belfry walls;
The tempest does not reach her shade,
    The rain her silent halls.

But sails are sweet in summer sky,
    The lark throws down a lay;
The long salt levels steam and dry,
    The cloud-heart melts away.

But patches of the sea-pink shine,
    The pied crows poise and come;
The mallow hangs, the bind-weeds twine,
    Where her sweet lips are dumb.

AN OCEAN GRAVE.

The passion of the wave is mute;
    No sound or ocean shock;
No music save the trilling flute
    That marks the curlew flock.

But yonder when the wind is keen,
    And rainy air is clear,
The merchant city's spires are seen,
    The toil of men grows near.

Along the coast-way grind the wheels
    Of endless carts of coal;
And on the sides of giant keels
    The shipyard hammers roll.

The world creeps here upon the shout,
    And stirs my heart in pain;
The mist descends and blots it out,
    And I am strong again.

Strong and alone, my dove, with thee;
    And, tho' mine eyes be wet,
There's nothing in the world to me,
    So dear as my regret.

I would not change my sorrow sweet
    For others' nuptial hours;
I love the daisies at thy feet
    More than their orange flowers.

My hand alone shall tend thy tomb,
    From leaf-bud to leaf-fall;
And wreathe around each season's bloom
    Till autumn ruins all.

Let snowdrops early in the year
    Droop o'er her silent breast;
And bid the later cowslip rear
    The amber of its crest.

AN OCEAN GRAVE.

Come hither, linnets tufted-red,
    Drift by, O wailing tern;
Set pure vale-lilies at her head,
    At her feet lady-fern.

Grow, samphire, at the tidal brink,
    Wave pansies of the shore,
To whisper how alone I think
    Of her for evermore.

Bring blue sea-hollies thorny, keen,
    Long lavender in flower;
Grey wormwood like a hoary queen,
    Stanch mullein like a tower.

O sea-wall mounded long and low,
    Let iron bounds be thine;
Nor let the salt wave overflow
    That breast I held divine.

AN OCEAN GRAVE.

Nor float its sea-weed to her hair,
    Nor dim her eyes with sands;
No fluted cockle burrow where
    Sleep folds her patient hands.

Tho' thy crest feel the wild sea's breath,
    Tho' tide-weight tear thy root,
Oh, guard the treasure-house, where death
    Has bound my darling mute.

Tho' cold her pale lips to reward
    With love's own mysteries,
Ah, rob no daisy from her sward,
    Rough gale of eastern seas!

Ah, render sere no silken bent,
    That by her head-stone waves;
Let noon and golden summer blent
    Pervade these ocean graves.

And, ah, dear heart, in thy still nest,
   Resign this earth of woes,
Forget the ardours of the west,
   Neglect the morning glows.

Sleep and forget all things but one,
   Heard in each wave of sea,—
How lonely all the years will run,
   Until I rest by thee.

OPHELIA.

Lost in a wilderness of ill,
Wan with a yearning never still,
O tell me where, most tuneful rill,
    Can I recover rest?

Thy waves roll under meadows brown,
And draw the thirsty daisies down;
It cannot hurt them much to drown,
    In death's green water-nest.

Among the meads of dædal May,
Around the roots of aspens grey,
Thy ripple holds delicious way,
    A couch where dreams are sweet;

OPHELIA.

Thy lilies shall my pillow be,
My coverlet the water free,
My sheet the white anemone,
    My lullaby thy beat.

Gone without warning otherwhere
My lover leaves me to despair;
Sorrow and love are sore to bear,
    Love goes and sorrow stays.

O father dead; O love untrue,
Lips at whose touch mine own grew new,
As pallid buds expand, if dew
    Drop after droughty days.

My father in his grave is fair,
The shroud is round his silver hair;
I love the hand that laid him there,
    And wrought my bosom's woe.

O pale dead father laid in night,
My bud of spring is slain with blight,
My soul is weary of the light
    And lonely; let her go.

I weep indeed; and both are gone—
Ah, most I love the cruel one,
Who loved me once, now loves me none,
    Dear author of my fears.

And so I wander by the brim,
And gather buds to think of him,
And find their eyes are dewy-dim,
    As mine are wan with tears.

The sad sweet avens as in dream,
Bends o'er the bosom of the stream,
And hangs her rosy head; I seem
    Like this deserted bloom.

The fishes watch her, amber-eyed,
The tide-grass swims from side to side,
As sweetly will the river glide,
    And kiss me in my tomb.

And he—God knows!—when nestlings break
Their eggs next summer, and the lake
Is sown with snowy hawthorn flake,—
    May wander one day here,

The darling of my troth and trust,
When he is crowned and I am dust,
May lean and weep—Ah, but he must—
    At least one little tear

Into my river-urn, when bees
Are roving, and the skies at peace,
And love, my pain, at ease, at ease,
    In my sweet water-bier!

SIGH, HEART, BREAK NOT.

SIGH, heart, and break not; rest, lark, and wake not!
Day I hear coming to draw my Love away.
As mere-waves whisper, and clouds grow crisper,
Ah, like a rose he will waken up with day.

In moon-light lonely, he is my Love only,
I share with none while Luna rides in grey.
As dawn-beams quicken, my rivals thicken,
The light and deed and turmoil of the day.

To watch my sleeper to me is sweeter,
Than any waking words my Love can say;
In dream he finds me and closer winds me!
Let him rest by me a little more and stay.

SIGH, HEART, BREAK NOT.

Ah, mine eyes close not: and, tho' he knows not,
    My lips on his be tender while you may;
Ere leaves are shaken, and ring-doves waken,
    And infant buds begin to scent new day.

Fair Darkness, measure thine hours, as treasure
    Shed each one slowly from thine urn, I pray;
Hoard in and cover each from my lover;
    I cannot lose him yet; dear night, delay.

Each moment dearer, true-love, lie nearer,
    My hair shall blind thee lest thou see the ray;
My locks encumber thine ears in slumber,
    Lest any bird dare give thee note of day.

He rests so calmly; we lie so warmly;
    Hand within hand, as children after play;—
In shafted amber on roof and chamber
    Dawn enters; my Love wakens: here is day.

SEPARATED FORTUNES.

Dearest, beholding thy poor married tears,
  Since thou hast made thy choice and chosen ill;
And I must watch the slow pathetic years
  Far from that hearth where thou art lonely still.

The cradle of thy sorrow claims thy care,
  O patient mother; on this mate of thine
Smile, if one careless word he has to spare;
  Crouch, if his hand be heavy with the wine.

I am slain with pity of thy doom to be.
  I pray; but easier shall this mountain gate
Unlock its roots and drench them in the sea,
  Than I could loose one rivet of thy fate.

SEPARATED FORTUNES.

Live; and thy child will grow to love thee right,
    The blighted years will rust themselves away;
Till to thy spirit weary for the night
    Sleep shall unroll the prison-doors of day.

I hear a noise of autumn round again;
    A few more seasons and we shall not weep.
We lived divided in our living pain;
    We shall lie sundered in our latest sleep.

Thou shalt repose where that Italian sea
    Rolls, without tide, more lucid than our waves.
By northern Humber's foam my rest shall be;
    The deep shall sound between us in our graves.

The moon at full will beam on either tomb;
    The stars at morn will hide themselves away.
No step will come more sadly for thy doom,
    No lark will sing less gaily in the grey.

Love in his end shall falter as did ours ;
   The true shall lose him and the traitor win.
Time as of old among life's garden flowers
   Shall pull as weeds the choicest buds therein.

Worn with her sentence of eternal blight
   Earth's seasons will not alter or rebel;
While up above the shining zenith-light
   They tell me Mercy sits—and all is well !

A RENUNCIATION.

Light of love and cold of brain,
    Shall I trust thy ready tears?
Shall I touch thine hand again
    As in light and childish years?
        Never! Ah, but this was sweet,
        To sigh worship at thy feet.

Lips as ripe have made men dust,
    Falsely gentle, many a one;
Adders I will sooner trust
    Than thy breasts; they cover stone.
        This is instinct with your sort,
        Ye must injure souls in sport.

A RENUNCIATION.

Prosper, while thy game is sure :
  Silly fishes haunt thy net.
Birds are busy round thy lure ;
  Curses will not catch thee yet.
    Run thy day ; inconstant thing,
    Dove in eyes and asp in sting.

Light thy lamp of fen-fire love ;
  There are fools enough to drown—
Me its ray shall never move,
  I at least have sat me down ;
    Proud is wrong ; I nurse my wound ;
    Leave me ; let the times roll round.

Wearied of thy glossy smile,
  Thro' its mask I seem to trace
Stern lips, cruel all the while
  On an artificial face,
    Dimpled over with death-snares,
    Whose eyes slay men unawares.

A RENUNCIATION.

Plough the rock and reap the sand.
Wear thy sickly smiles for gain.
Blight the lips that touch thy hand;
Years thy hireling cheek will stain:
Love will lay thee on his shelf,
Left, mean torment, to thyself!

THE RED-BREAST.

My red-breast, continue thy song beyond seasons
   When the passage bird's mad lay is over and past;
Pipe sweet to my lady and trill her my reasons;
   Be thy note weak as dew she will harken at last.

Alder droops and the aspen rocks as the year closes,
   The daisy roots shiver expecting the snows.
As autumn and equinox alter the roses,
   Reason with her, pretty bird, as it blows.

Tell her the emblem of leaves as they wither;
   Lay at her feet broken buds, perished fruit;
Whisper my darling, that all things drift thither,
   Where the lips of the queens of Love's garden are
      mute.

For the wood-bee has garnered his cells with bloom-
    harvest,
And among his sweet wealth he is drowsy and dumb.
For the squirrel has hidden, ere weather bite sharpest,
    His acorns and beech-nuts as latter rains come.

O my child, there is age, there is death; each a spectre;
    One will wither, one whiten thy cheek's elfin rose;
Garner then, as a wise bee, some store of Love's nectar
    To cherish thy heart in its seasons of snows!

RETROSPECT.

If we have pondered on a face,
   In yonder age of simple days,
If burning lips of first embrace
   Sealed us as pilgrims in love's ways—

The silly chains became us well,
   When rosy lay the orchard roods,
And April buds began to swell,
   And starlings thought about their broods.

The easy fetters bound us sweet;
   The shrill lark dwindled overhead.
The land lay incense at our feet.
   We did not dream upon the dead!

RETROSPECT.

With ardent cheek and earnest breath
    We plighted unenduring vows;
And bound, instead of amaranth wreath,
    Deciduous roses round our brows.

Bud after bud descends to dust;
    Those rare years sigh and go their way.
We leave our garlands, since we must,
    When heads begin to gather grey.

Then farewell, Love, for other skies,
    We laud thee now we need thee least.
We will not be as guests, who rise
    And, risen, chide against a feast.

Untainted we will always save
    The sweet of thy memorial joy;
Let fools thy royal table leave
    And soil the banquet with alloy.

Go, harpy, with thy loathsome wing,
　Go, cynic, with thy touch of mire!
We hold it an ignoble thing
　To laugh against our old desire;

Ye seem to scorn Love's richer hour,
　In envy half, but more in craft,
And wholly sullen: since your flower
　Is withered on its autumn shaft.

We least will ape this dotard's part,
　Who sneers at love in aspen tone,
Who jests on his once wholesome heart,
　And cheapens all who still have one.

He hárdens in his selfish crust;
　His blear eyes only understand
Three things as comely—wine, and lust,
　And greed which guides the palsied hand.

RETROSPECT.

Irreverent, isolated thing!
   Old scare-crow on the field of vice,
Some rags of youth around thee cling
   To flutter in a land of ice!

Leave in his shrine, veiled round and sad,
   The Amor of thy tender days.
Thank Heaven that once thou couldst be glad,
   Be silent, if thou canst not praise.

Ah, crush not in with tainted feet:
   Is thy thought cankered, keep away.
Tho' idols snap, and fair things fleet,
   Leave one spot pure wherein to pray.

Some day indeed, before thy last,
   When all life's boughs are bare of fruit,
When mock and sneer are overpast,
   And every shallow laugh is mute.

Come to this haven, and unveil
    The imaged face thy youth held best,
Kneel down before it, have thy wail,
    And crawl the better to thy rest.

AN AUTUMN SERENADE.

BEFORE the tears of autumn shed
    All leaves away at winter's door,
My queen, across the foliage tread
    Of yellow gusty woodland floor;
And watch the squirrel overhead
    In stories of her pine-trees hoar.

When only redbreast chirps thee on,
    And fingered chestnut leaves are cast;
And gaudy greenwood gathers wan
    On lime and beech, and sickens fast;
And acorns thicken paths upon,
    And shrew-mice treasure winter mast.

AN AUTUMN SERENADE.

When plovers tremble up to cloud,
 And starling legions whirl apace;
And redwing nations restless-loud
 Are over every fallow's face;
And barren branches like a shroud
 Blacken the sun-way's interspace.

The winds, all summer idly dead,
 Give prelude to their winter tune.
Grey hoar-frost hears them, from his bed
 Lays out white hands, and wakens soon.
He laughs as soughing elm-trees shed
 Old homes of breeding rooks in June.

A FAREWELL.

Since thy lips hunger to pronounce farewell,
    And a pale mist makes bitter both our faces,
Tear down the banner on Love's citadel,
    Lead up the rabble to his pleasant places.

Go to thy Siren, she is fresh and white;
    My love is worn; oblivion is its meed.
Let her ray darken mine with ampler light;
    I, in her zenith dwindle and recede.

Let her round arms be as the sun-way is,
    More sweet than all old kisses her last one;
Lest I should weep, I will consider this,
    Love once came in our dreams; he is well gone!

And yet my thought is busy on one dream,
    Now I am stranded past the reach of tide,—
Imagine, whither, had I held the stream,
    Love would have helmed us in his boat to glide.

Again the rocking current draws our keel,
    The sun is nearer and the moon more fair,
Our pilot Love, beneath whose rosy heel
    As dust are laid empire and time and care.

Arcadian spaces of great grass arise;
    Crisp lambs are merry: hoary vales are laid,
Studded with roe-deer and wild straw-berries:
    In one a shepherd tabours, near a maid,

Who teazes at the button of his cloak,
    Where rarely underneath them grows the herb;
A squirrel eyes the lovers from an oak,
    And speckled horses pasture without curb.

A FAREWELL.

In a fair meadow set with tulip heads;
    A water-mill rolls little crested falls
Of olive torrent, broken in grey threads,
    A grave-yard crowds black crosses in square walls.

Quaint pastoral Arcadia, where are set
    Thy rainy lands and reddish underwoods?
Earth hath not held thy fabled sunsets yet,
    Though lovers build their palace on thy roods.

My Love in dream was changeless: he of earth,
    A changeling god unstable as the sand,
Reckons his gifts and reasons in his mirth:
    His kisses! a child counts them on one hand.

Under his instep once arose light flowers,
    Now dead and curled, as leaves in caverns dry,
Where heedless gusts have lost them at odd hours;
    So out of sight time pushes loves gone by.

A FAREWELL.

Time held Love's daughter fair a little while;
    Wept at her feet and died at her desire;
He would have bartered heaven for one sweet smile,
    But now her roses are as highway mire.

O child of change, thy refuge is "farewell;"
    The dumb slow days teach many, may teach thee.
I shall not lure Love back with any spell;
    Soiled are his feet, his hand rough, let him flee!

Leave to the kingdom of thy new delight,
    A land of vines and apples overhead;
Where the great golden stars move out at night,
    And the air burns with love when day is dead.

Let her await thee, thy new Siren, there,
    This garden-empress, thy most beautiful;
Whose robe is red as sun-death, and her hair
    Gleams as the rippled eve-cloud wonderful.

A FAREWELL.

Seal up thy past with kisses, lest a cry,
    A shape, a phantom, in thy lightest hour
With dead sad eyes and wandering arms go by,
    And turn the vintage of thy passion sour.

Till on thy lips the red wine savour blood,
    And garlands grind as ashes on thy head ;
And loathly tastings taint thy banquet food,
    And marriage guests seem mourners of the dead.

Ah, for Remorse is mighty, blind thy soul,
    And hoop thine heart with iron to forget,
Drown Record under ocean's tidal roll,
    And deeper than an oak-root hide Regret.

Wind rough acanthus round thy burning cup,
    Let white arms soothe thee and fresh lips of song,
Lie sweetly down and rise in gladness up,
    Quench—*if thou canst*—the echo of my wrong !

THE CARDINAL'S LAMENT.

ROME: EASTER DAY, 1872.

O PERFECT bride of God, renew thy tears;
Waken, my Rome, my chosen; feel the chains
Around thy sacred limbs; the iron weighs
Thy sweet hand earthward: lonely art thou bound,
In fetters, Rome, a mighty broken queen,
Staring with wild eyes at the Easter dawn—
Thro' all the night most patient till the ray—
The awful dumb dead night, wherein the Lord's
White body lay, with red wounds of the nails,
Waiting the resurrection touch to move;
And all the watcher angels o'er his shroud
Held awful silence, dim among the gloom,
Nor dared to stir or rustle any wing!

In hope they waited ; we have watched in none.
Lo ! yonder sailing mist of signal rose
Is Easter, our celestial rising-day—
Easter in Rome, where Easter meant so much,
And drew the world a pilgrim ; where men deemed
Her gorgeous consecrations here on earth
Some foretaste of the festival in Heaven.

Beautiful sleeps the city in her mist.
Still are the fountains, calm her mighty squares,
Untrodden all her labyrinth of ways.
The very doves are silent and asleep
That build about St. Peter's. All the trees
In the Pope's garden seem blurred heads of cloud.
The great dome looms dull brown, unburnished yet ;
Beneath whose soundless aisles in glory sleep
The dead Popes in their order, pale and still
And patient till the coming of their Christ ;
That Easter of all graves, when Christ shall call
To his doom-angel, " Blow, the hour is ripe,
And ended is the sorrow of my own,

And ready is my sentence on the dead ;
I have completed all my saints, and come.
Gather the nations. I will judge and end !"

Come ! for the earth is heavy, and we mourn.
Ah, spare us many Easters like this last ;
For now the ungodly chide at us, and say,
We have no Christ this Easter to arise,
We watch corruption by some common grave,
Our Christ is in the ground, he will not hear.
We are dreamers, how in some old fabled tale,
A good man died unjustly, lay in earth,
How soldiers sealed the cavern of his rest :
How lovely dawned that Easter, when of old
The Galilean women came to weep,
Loving the gentle prophet that was gone.
So far the tale is credible : but now
We hear of certain angels, when indeed
Philosophy has settled there were none.
We hear of how the cold dead Christ arose—

But one wise Frenchman wrote a pretty book,
And proved that dead men always fell to dust.

So they blaspheme the watchers at thy grave—
Ah, God, the infidel is master here.
Here in thy Rome, thy last Jerusalem,
Thy righteous rose, the city of thy priests.
Is it well seen, O God? The abominable
Hath circled us weak fishes with his net.
His chain is on thy vicar, lord of stars;
The prisoner father droops in lonely halls,
The purple princes of the conclave weep.
While northern vermin, exiles, Piedmontese,
Scum of the alp-root, turn the holy town
To one vast barrack-yard of noisy war;
Set sentinels, have beacons, order camps,
Clatter along our squares, blow horns, beat drums;
Until the voices of our rhythmic bells
Are shamed to silence in a place of siege,
And mighty Rome lies dumb without a word.

THE CARDINAL'S LAMENT.

Behold a trumpet from the Capitol
Calls through the shallow vapour of the dawn.
"The night in heaven is done, but not in Rome,
Her eyes are tender to sustain the sun—
She loves her prison-shadows more than day."
A bugle answers from the Palatine,
"Great Rome is vanquished, fallen. We have come
And conquered the impregnable, the joy
Of God, the lamp of nations. At her gates
We rode, and blew a careless blast and won.
She is bound, we have bound her, we!"

     And who are these,
Who call so proudly out of Cæsar's nest?
"We are Italians and have conquered Rome."
If ye indeed be sons of Italy,
Ye are risen against your mother, with foul hands
Ye have smitten upon your parent's holy face,
Ye have bruised her sacred lips until they bleed:
Your hands are red: ask pardon on your knees.

THE CARDINAL'S LAMENT.

"She turned a tyrant, therefore is she bound;
Turin hath conquered Rome." O deed of shame!
The weazel triumphs in the wolf-cub's lair.
Shall Rome hew Piedmont's wood, go to the well
For Piedmont; fetch and carry, as she's told,
Take buffets in the service of this thing?
Rome with her grand commemorative past,
Searching her annals, reading on her tombs,
Hath only heard of Piedmont yesterday;
As pasture of some hunger-bitten cows
Fed in the misty alp-heart up in heaven;
A realm of neat-herds, frozen in the cold.
Are these thy spoilers, city of the sun,
At whose great royal breasts the baby mouths
Of emperors drew nurture? Is this thou,
Whose mother-vein abounding gave to these
Their after strength to bruise and break the world?
Thy power was on them and they overcame,
And meted out the immeasurable earth
Among the purple nurslings of their loins.

THE CARDINAL'S LAMENT.

Thy yesterdays, my Rome, are wonderful,
But awful change hath snapt thee in its snare,
With iron edge of strange calamities.
Bring down, my queen, thy bosom on the dust,
Shame thy bright hair with ashes; be their slave,
This hungry tribe of ragged mountaineers,
Who drape themselves in robes that Brutus wore,
And say, "We are Italy!" Return, keep cows,
Bring fodder in. Ye are herdsmen, brutish, boors!
Our common earth is nobler than your lives,
Our soil is mingled with imperial dust,
Our city is one catacomb of kings.
Begone! your feet defile your masters' grave.
But your realm rose a mushroom in the night,
Sardinians. "Nay," ye answer, "we are risen,
Being the sons of progress in the south;
Ours is the 'liberal' kingdom, typifies
The new emergence of the baby-world
To ampler knowledge. Turin with her heel
Upon Rome's neck, means old theology

THE CARDINAL'S LAMENT.

Prostrate before philosophy's new dawn;
Victor in Rome means light in the human soul—
But you, who blame our Piedmont, have good heed,
You with the tonsure, teacher of the folds,
Priest, prophet, in whatever name or robe,
You lead God man-ward, and raise men to God—
Behold, to all your sort the crucial hour
Arrives, the world-child strengthens out its limbs,
The papmeat season never can return.
Cleanse your religion clean of mythic lore,
Heave out old forms and fables to the deep.
The peoples roar for reasonable meat,
Keen they discern the draff among the food;
Humour their fancies else they will away;
The sheep will crawl for pasture to the wolf;
And leave you droning mass in empty fanes,
And tear the titles to your revenues.
Therefore, O priest, chop science with the best,
Cram us with reason, demonstrate, convince,
Avoid all dogma, or apologise

If gritty Athanasian bits protrude.
Lead us in roads historically laid,
Well lamped at intervals, without a rut
To jog the queasy conscience into doubt.
Then quietly thy sheep in tribes shall come,'
And tinkle after with obedient bleats
Him with the crook, the triple cap, and keys.
Hold to the causeway Reason; Faith's a slough
On either hand. One tread, you're ankle-deep,
The next inextricably over-ears.
The flock forbade its pastor to diverge,
So far as hoof bit rock it followed him;
Here it tried footing, sniffed, and halted dead;
He blundered on, the quagmire sucked him in;
His woolbacks move without him; serve him righ'!'

Which is a parable! and comes to this,—
An evil people, greedy of a sign,
Must comprehend to worship, analyse
Ere they adore. Each individual soul

With his small lanthorn walks the world alone;
He lifts no eyes on heaven's high fitful stars;
Indeed he cannot kindle or relume
Those large white lamps of God; a rush-light's best,
Whose feeble sputtering insignificance
You trim yourself to grapple with the gloom.

Ye blind and lonely feelers in the dark,
Ye halt men arrogant, ye wise run mad,
Who shall provide such gropers with a god,
Before what essence will ye bend your knees?
Believe in Euclid, worship axioms,
Trust in triangles, to a cube sing hymns!
I see no other worship for the fools.

Have ye not understood, ere time began
Reason and Faith have been unreconciled?
Their feud is old as ocean, keen as fire;
As oil and acid mingle so do they.
You cannot build a reasonable faith.

THE CARDINAL'S LAMENT.

Vain is your labour, if you rear a wall
And smear no mortar in between the chinks.
Ah, teacher, build thy little tower of cards.
Try! Meet all views, prune, sift, avoid old sores,
Tread upon no man's theologic corns;
Frame some mild creed with neither back nor bones,
A mist of genial benevolences
To please all round, Budd, Calvin, Moses, Comte.
Fair bodes the scheme in its first fluid stage,—
It makes a tidy pamphlet, well reviewed,—
But crystallize it can't, except around
Some little tiny notion of a god,
Some germ organic in the central haze
To vivify and quicken the inert;
Some atom-grain of personality
To sweeten and begin a crust of rays.

Here your dilemma rises, man of mind.
Either ignore your god-mote, leave your scheme
A vapid thing to fester on grey shelves,

THE CARDINAL'S LAMENT.

Limp, theoretic, leprous, flat, inane;
Or accept something which transcends your rules,
And promulgate your germ-god's attributes;
Till by degrees your wary pen grows warm,
And the third column of your monograph
Lands you in purest dogma half-way down;
Then the pace strengthens, acrid, on you flow
Till *finis* dubs you scientific pope,
Damning opponents all to left or right,
As idiots or as rascals. Rome herself
Ne'er fulminated deeper. Hold, my friend:
Remember where we started; reason and sight,
All else you rolled away. Where are we now?

Your fairest hope is, you may frame at best,
An almost credible theology.
Alas, wise man, that "almost" ruins all,
It means you postulate one thing on trust;
Be it the least division of a hair,
One fibre in a gnat; confession's made

That some faith's wanted. Faith, say, in a midge.
Concede me this—I answer, then believe
In Juggernaut and all his monstrous heads;
Size is no test to the deductive brain;
In each the mental process is the same.
Neither the gnat nor idol can be proved,
You took the midge on trust, accept the god !

The nations are as children, after all;
Some blind, some blinkard. You or I of these
See by some inches further than our nose.
I grant our reason's keener, but what then?
The contradictions in the simplest creed,
The reasonablest revelation known,
Are to our wits and those of country clods
An equal wall of nonsense. We are lithe,
And they are lame, but Atlas intervenes,
And neither can o'erleap his barrier rocks.
Inform a drayman two and two are five,
He stares and lounges on. Repeat the lie

THE CARDINAL'S LAMENT.

To some great thinker gravely, he growls out,
"Disturb me not; return, O dunce, to school."
Suppose God said, "Believe that two straight lines
Could hedge a space in; be convinced of this,
Or miserably perish. On this truth
My church is founded. All who contradict
Are lost throughout the abysses of all time."
Will reason help you here? You shudder. No.
Dismiss the fancy, and compare the fact.
How hath the just God spoken? He hath bound
All nations at their peril to receive,
That perfect God was also perfect man.
Digest this truth by reason, if you may;
Reason won't aid; at faith arrive you must
Sooner or later; and if you take in
One grain by faith which reason cannot chew,
You may as well swallow a mountain down,
And lay all doubt asleep, and rest your brains
And conscience in a comfortable church;
Nor let the devils lash you out to the hills

To chop dry logic in the barren cold,
Beneath the stern inexorable stars.

What follows? Has God left the world quite dark?
Have all the ages tumbled men to hell
Along the lampless ledges of the past?
Pitiful souls, whose reason led them wrong.
Is there no beacon ready till the dawn,
No light his love hath saved us? Blind, behold
His affluence dwells among us; and ye turn
And answer, "Show us God and it's enough."
Lo, Peter's chair, and God in flesh thereon!

Refuse the truth, hale down his vicar's throne,
Lead back the lees of Rome to mock and spit
At the old venerable saint, whose locks
Are white with many winters of long prayer,
Whose hand is weak with blessing men so long,
Whose kind eyes sadden at your ruffian deeds.
Are ye come up with tumult to destroy?

To quench our only light and leave the world
Eyeless and dark—as here our Easter is.
Destruction is so easy.   God allows
The fiends to overturn, that they may feel
Horrible hell around them when all's done,
And awful isolation from their deed.

But, ah, ye errant peoples of God's fold,
How would this holy foster-mother Rome,
Have gathered you between her ample wings,
And called you in beneath her silken plumes,
And yet ye would not.   Her sweet house and ours
Is surely left unto us desolate ;
And God's own chosen flower, celestial Rome,
Is chained lamenting in her Easter dawn.*

---

* The sentiments expressed in this monologue are those of the Cardinal and not of the writer. Surely, such an intimation is unnecessary : yet a critic with some experience of our reading public thinks otherwise.

MEDEA.

A TRAGEDY OF JEALOUSY.

(DRAMATIC FRAGMENT.)

Medea.

Why dost thou wrong and shame me more each day?
What have I done to merit this disdain?
Declare the measure of my injuries;
Publish my fault, O perjured; ere I cry
To Zeus, that presently he cleave thy brain
With one keen hissing bundle of blue fire;
And Artemis may heave her spear on me,
If I be found unfaithful in her sight
By one least errant thought to this hard man!
Thine answer, king, thy reason; say them soon.

The King.

Nay, for I will not answer; get her in,
Who was a queen and is a Mænad now,
A raving woman smitten with wild gods;
A Pythoness in wreaths of sulphur fume,
Perplexed with inward voices terrible—
Is this a royal fashion to bewail,
To ring out curses wildly in the air,
To entreat and clench numb fingers in the dust?
Roll up thy Bacchanalian hair; begone!

Chorus.

In ashes she has laid her shining head;
Give her the answer of a little word;
Leave wrath to Zeus and to his gods revenge:
Indeed, she is angry, broken, dumb with sighs!

Medea.

With sighs I think that I have nearly done,
With grief and seed of sighs and fruit of tears,
Done with the earth crowned over with blown woods,
Done with her shadowed vales and sleepy fields.

With the wave rocking and high glorious stars—
I have concluded surely with them all;
And in my distance only one dark gate,
Rent in the rock and fringed with deadly yew,
Invites my lonely feet. I will descend,
Laden with many curses at thy hand,
Along its blind and miserable road,
Hollow, uneven, rugged, arduous,
Into that realm, where Love and wrong of him
Seem like our tears in childhood. I will go;
Let railing cease and trivial anger fall.
I will obey my tyrant and depart.
Yet one small bitter word I mean to speak
Under my breath, not very loud or wild,
Yet some far god will hear it in his heaven;
And see thou to it, king, if answer come.

Chorus.

Revere, O king, her curse and answer it;
Curses are strong; they climb as ravens up
Vexing the easy and complacent gods,

To feed them and fulfil them; inmost heaven
Is weary with their wail and sounding wings;
The drowsy brows of the eternal ones
Move in their rest to frown and sleep again;
Till the great angry Zeus shall prop himself
Wide-eyed upon his elbow, roused at last,
And toss a plague upon thy realm and thee,
To have about him quiet heaven again.
Therefore, O king, be mild and give reply,
Nor stand apart with dull eyes on the ground,
And dumb hard lips. But royally she comes
To speak and raises out her angry arms.

Medea.

Ye damsels of this land, when I am dead,
Search me some grave secluded; where the step
Of that light foolish woman, whom he loves,
May never beat mine ashes. Here engrave
Around my tomb in yellow characters
The fair deeds of this hero to his spouse.
How for a season with man's fickle love

He gave me adoration as his queen;
And loved me fairly once—as these men love!
The sorrow of my kingdom faded me;
To be at once a mother and a queen
Is care enough, and beauty wanes in care.
Then he began to scorn my haggard eyes,
And found their light no longer eloquent;
For many watchings at the cradle head
Drew dimness, where love's glory used to burn—
As least he said so once. All that is gone!
So, of this pale face weary, he found one
More rosy to his mind, a captive wench,
Silly enough and fresh enough to please
The veering tyrant. Folded in my robes,
She struts about the palace at his side,
Aping the queen with gestures of the plough;
And my unstable hand-maids bow to her
When he is near, and mock her when he goes;
Help as they are to none, weak water-waves,
That point their heads as each wind pushes them.

And me they counsel to wink hard at this,
Ignoring my desertion, to look sweet
And speak him smooth, and, hypocrite, refrain,
Until this alien fancy's turn is done;
And then to kiss and make it up again.
Ah, God, not so. I will be all with him
Or nothing; no dumb slave with pleasant lips,
While glowing embers at her bosom's core
Eat out her heart. O perjured husband, nay,—
I, firm in this my wife-hood, a chaste bride,
In old love blameless, choose not to survive
This infamy of wedlock; so I wend
Beneath the mighty darkness all alone,
Unreconciled and homeless. As my home
Is the new Love's to rule in, and my lord
Glooms on his children as a step-father
Turned by this rose-red fool against his own;
And I pray Zeus to bring into my brain
Strong words and bitter potency of curse,
Against my marriage bed and its ill fruit,

That I may blare them out and die at ease.

Chorus.

Strong is thy seat, O monarch, as the sun;
And what is weaker than a woman's tear?
Yet rear her from the ground. The ancient gods
Are fickle if one prosper overmuch;
Calamity has broken many thrones.

King.

Why this is brave; must I a king endure
The windy ravings of a woman's ire,
Must I teach reason to her, mad with whims?
Must a king bend his eyes into his cloak,
And give no maiden greeting in the street?
Must he go dumbly, tied to one queen's heels,
Where she in strings may lead him up and down,
A craven laughter to the market-wives
Above their baskets? Threat me not with Zeus,
He has a railing queen to curb at home;
Call thou on Hêrê; Zeus will help thee none,
He is well sick of married jealousies.

Medea.

Thy word is well, and so shall rise my prayer,
I will indeed entreat this Zeus no more;
I will call up beyond him to a god
Mightier than he, a shadow dimly known,—

Chorus.

Refrain, O queen, for awful words as these;
I veil my head in fear as they are said.

Medea.

O thou beyond the darkness and the cloud,
How can I make my call, how bring my prayer?
Can I appeal, strange even to thy name?
Are not these very weak words that I speak
Wrung from my heart like blood, tear after tear?
Wilt thou, O terrible, hear any one?
Are our tears pleasant, is our bleeding sweet
Before thee? Are the striving, and the void,
The throb, and this blind reaching out of hands,
Excellent music or unheeded noise?
Thou hast made Love, else hadst thou nothing made,

Else had the unformed silence still endured,—
Is not Love rightly cruel as thyself?
Love thou hast made, and beautiful it is,
A dream of many lights and shaken waters,
Excellent, unenduring, human Love!

Chorus.

It is a dreadful daring to beat out
New roads of prayer. So many gods are known,
Eager of knees, of kine insatiable.
In every field a flameless altar stands
Greedy of sacrifice. Ah, kindle one.
Numberless temples glisten in the groves,
The thrones in roomy heaven are full of gods;
Choose and invoke one hand of many arms
Able to pluck thee from thy coil of storms.
Let some god of thy fathers oar thy soul
To haven. Hold thy fingers on thy teeth;
Offer no incense to this nameless one.
Dumb lips indeed were aid as good as his,
And silence the best censer in thy palm.

Fate and not God has made thy path to bear
Flint at thy soles and at thy instep briers.

King.

She is full of dreams and rumours and reproof,
She is folded in the bands of bitter pride;
Hard-eyed as death, as unpersuadable,
Deaf to the deaf winds let her wail aloud—
In this thy storm remember thou art queen.
The fury of thy anger overthrows
Thine honour and my patience. Are thy wrongs,
If any, sweeter for unrolling them
Here in broad day before a herd of slaves?
If thou be wounded tend thy hurt at home.
If woe be come on thee, it rightly came;
Yet here I tell no reasons why it grew,
Being a king and guarding my reserve.
Then, on thine honour, which, O queen, is mine,
Control this common phrenzy, and return
Indoors; upon thy duty as a spouse,
By thy maternal love, I charge thee—Go!

Medea.

Let me be very patient and most meek—
Consider this, ye women, mark it well;
He, even this man perjured, prates of love,
Is wounded in his honour, finds me slack
In wifely duty; come, complete my wrong
And make it perfect; bring thy paramour
Here in my face to teach me how I fail.
This toy of milk and rosebuds, this new girl
Without a purpose and without a soul,
Save to live sleek and whiten her smooth skin,
The slavish plaything of a banquet hour.
Why she would never stand an hour in the rain
To serve the man who loved her; ay, and men
Have fallen to such loving, pure men too—
If she presume to school me in my love,
My soul, let us be patient even in this.
The shadow of the blood which I have shed,
The tumult of the years that I have ruled,
Have never touched her in her rose-garden.

She cannot dream the woman that I am,
This doll fit only to be kissed and fed,
To chide and chatter, pout and start aside
At the first trumpet-note of danger and death,
Screaming and useless, tossed as lumber by.
Then, as thou reachest for thy spear, my Lord,
Wilt thou find counsel at her pretty lips?
Toss her away till thou hast stemmed the storm
Then, if thou wilt, return and kiss again
Her cheeks to colour. Surely she is meet
To be a hero's wife. O stars of god,
I have known many women brave and pure,
Worthy of kings and wifedom, true and leal;
And in their number she will never come;
Slave, if thou wilt, and concubine enough,
Not wife nor near it. Else this feeble trash
Would shame us out of wifehood with her fears.
Yet, O my lord, my only Love, my King,
Altho' the light I found in thy dear eyes
Wanes, and thou standest ever coldly apart;

Tho' to my dumb entreating hands and eyes
I gain no answer. Tho' the father's face
Harden against our children. Tho' I lose
Thy presence day by day, and evermore
Thou makest any pretext to begone—
Still let me nurse once more my child to rest,
As in old days beside thee; one swift hour
Endure me; make pretence that all is well,
Lest the child suffer; sit with me a little
Just now and then. I am old, I know, and faded,
I never had much youth! Our years have been
So stormy; husband, how you loved me then!
How sweet it was to tread the brinks of death,
One will between us. O we went so firmly:
I felt thy hand upon my hand, and fear
Became a laughter. Thro' the smoke of death,
The dragon land, the fiery deeps of blood,
I saw one face—my husband's—and went on,
As tho' I felt the daisies at my feet
In meadow places under quiet woods.

It is my glory to have been thy mate,
Not idle, but another living brain
Building thy throne beside thee, night and day ;
In rumours of conspiracy, in hours
Of chidden armies, still at thy right hand
Undaunted ; when rebellion, bolt by bolt,
Played round our royal heads to tear us down ;
Did I quail then, did I seem pitiful?
Not so, men said, this woman is all steel,
But they were wrong, I was all love ; no more.
My husband was my law and law-giver,
And righteous any deed that helped him best.
I bathed my hands in carnage and was glad ;
For every stain of blood upon my robes
Had seated him securer on his throne,
Who was my sun in heaven, my oracle,
My breath, my soul, my justice.   Hear me now,
When the long dark is ready for my feet ;
Love, husband, master, king, almost my God,
In whose dear service my whole life a slave

Has bent herself adoring. I required
Only a little love as my reward;
On this my soul was nourished, only on this—
Now he despises, scorns, and spits at me;
Smiles on that other woman, whom he loves,
And clothes her in all glory, once my own;
Whereby I weep all night, and only rise
To tears—tears—tears; and I discern no end,
Save the cold common grave where I descend.

Semi-chorus.

The sullen king turns roughly on his heel,
Whirling his regal mantle round his eyes,
And so departs with slow steps, obstinate.
Ah, but the queen, the pale one, beautiful,
Prone, in the dust her holy bosom laid,
Mingles her out-spread hair with fallen leaves,
And sandal-soil is on her gracious head.
Ah, lamentable lady, pitiful!
On to an altar in the palace court
She, crawling, interlaces nerveless hands.

Attend, her lips are twitching into prayer;
Listen, indeed there is no sound in them,
Only a choking murmur unlike words.
Bring out her children here, unclasp her arms
And raise her. It is done. The babies lie.
Smiling up into her hard vacant eyes,
One playing with her hair. But she stares on
In ecstasy, and cannot tell her own.
O miserable mother bring her in;
Since I discern the storm-drops on these flags,
And clouds are rough with thunder overhead.

Chorus.

  Sweet are the ways of death to weary feet,
    Calm are the shades of men.
  The phantom fears no tyrant in his seat,
    The slave is master then.

  Love is abolished; well, that this so;
    We knew him best as Pain.

The gods are all cast out, and let them go,
    Who ever found them gain?

Ready to hurt and slow to succour these;
    So, while thou breathest, pray.
But in the sepulchre all flesh has peace;
    Their hand is put away.

NATURE'S RENEWING.

THE genial year awakening,
   When mellow air begins to burn,
Arises in a robe of spring
   From ruined winter's hoary urn;
Whom hearing, all dumb birds must sing.

The sacred earth in her delight
   Steams under April's wheeling sun.
The king-cup gathers amber might,
   The clouds in triumph melt and run.
The grey lark trembles out of sight.

And here and there a fervid bud,
   The restless herald of the year,

When vernal currents move its blood,
    Expands in painted petals clear.
The flushed merle screams along the wood.

The rain is tender on the ground.
    Smooth-headed robins ruffle out
Their plumage.   Spring, in every sound
    Divine and sudden, sheds about
Her green dilation at a bound.

The sap in old blind things is warmed :
    The eager palm outruns its leaves.
The peering crocus, turf-embalmed,
    In gardens under cottage eaves
Comes now the hollow winds are calmed.

Those faint red boles with many a line,
    Those peeling sides, the ring-dove's perch,
Which white in darkened coppice shine
    Are silver clusters of the birch ;
They seem bright woodland ladies fine !

NATURE'S RENEWING.

The larch has blushing finger-tips;
   As tho' love-whispers of the spring
Had reached her on the March-winds' lips,
   Or she had heard them in the ring
Of rain-drops down the forest slips.

And in the wasted snow-drop's room
   Come daffodils abundantly,
The treasure of the violet's gloom
   Dividing with her. Can they be,
Those steady purples aspen bloom?

O glory of the dim green bough,
   O April floors of primrose zone:
It seems as if the grey world now
   Had laid asleep her ocean moan,
And barren drifts of windy snow.

JAEL.

So then their hymn of victory is done.
Thank God for that. Home are the soldiers gone.
The garlands of the triumph wither brown,
The singing-girls are sleepy, the hoarse crowd
Murmurs itself away. Night rises fast.
The shadows on the canvass of my tent
Deepen, and Jael in her lonely home
Begins to think it over, now the blare
Of clarions do not hail her longer blest.
O lying voice! Methought, I found a crown
Of glory, silvern : out I held my hand
And drew a burnished adder off her nest,
Who stung me redly first, and, when blood dried,
In one small pit of poison deadly-blue.
The name of that ill worm is Infamy.
So the moon comes and silence in her train ;
There will not be a many stars to-night.
The wind begins his circuit with a wail.

He tastes and touches at each little peak,
And in the broken furrows like a bird
Sings out in darkness. Why art thou so sad?
"O blessed among women"—So they sang
With brazen lips to God. But he knows more
And with one great chain binds my heavy soul;
I do not think that God will ever reach
His finger down and ease it. He hates me;
You see, I cannot weep. Does that sound well?
How many evil women can find tears,
Sinning all day. My one great deed of blood
Outweighs, as Horeb, in the scales of God
Against some petty sand-grains. He sees that,
Insists upon it, keeps it in his books
In plain red flaring letters that endure.
These women have a hundred petty ways
Of sinning feebly. He forgets them all.
They sin as ants or flies. He cannot praise
Or blame such creatures, simply lets them be.
I feel all this alone with my own heart.

The solitude is busy with God's voice
Speaking my sin. I am worn and wearied out;
A mere weak woman, after all is said;
Searching the intense dark with sleepless eyes,
Huddled away by the main-pole in the midst,
A curled crushed thing, a blurred white heap of robes,
Moaning at times with wild arms reaching out.
While on my canvass walls the rain-gush comes,
And the ropes scream and tighten in the blast.

So I must watch until my lord return;
The camp of Israel holds to-night carouse,
And Heber sits at Barak's own right hand;
Because I have risen against a sleeping man,
And slain him, like a woman. No man slays
After this sort. The craven deed is mine,
Hold thou its honour, Heber; have thy wine.
Among the captains claim the noblest seat;
And revel, if thou hast the heart, till dawn,
Brave at the board and feeble in the field!

JAEL.

As the sun fell this eve I felt afraid,
For in his fading, as he touched the haze,
I saw in heaven one round ripe blot of blood.
And all the gates of light, whereby he died,
Were wasted to one drop, a crimson seed;
I turned away and made mine eyelids fast;
But deep down in my soul I saw it still
The single reddish clot. The blood was pale;
They say pale blood is deadlier than the red,
And pallid this one drop. I think it came
Out of his forehead underneath the nail.
I had been told that slain men bled so much,
I nerved my soul for rivers and none flowed.
Somehow, his bloodless death was awfullest.
There seemed no reason, why at one swift blow
Of my deft hands this warm flushed sleepy man
Should cease into a statue, as he did,
At one shock of the hammer on his brow.
(I heard a fable once,—a trader's tale,
Who sailed from Javan's islands hawking veils—

How with a mallet one struck stone to flesh;
He was a cunning carver, if he did;
But I smote flesh to marble. That's no skill,
Requires a devil only.)   He turned once—
Twice—with a sort of little heaving moan,
A strange sad kind of choking under-sound;
And opened at me full great piteous eyes,
Already glazing with reproachful films;—
As with one gasp—I fancy he gasped twice—
He lay there done with, that great goodly man;
And in his sidelong temple, where bright curls
Made crisp and glorious margin to his brows—
So that a queen might lay her mouth at them
Nor rise again less royal for their kiss—
There, in the interspace of beard and brow,
The nail had gone tearing the silken skin;
And, driven home to the jagged head of it,
Bit down into the tent-boards underneath;
And riveted that face of deadly sleep;
As some clown nails an eagle on his barn,

JAEL.

The noble bird slain by the ignoble hand,
So slept the lordly captain at my feet;
His lovely eyes were hardly troubled now;
Yet in his keen grey lips a certain scorn
Dwelt as indignant, that a deed so mean,
Treason so petty, woman-guile so poor,
Should ever stifle out their glorious breath.
As I leant o'er them their serene disdain
Was eloquent against me, more than words,
And easy was the meaning of their scorn
To render and interpret into this—
" Better to be as we are earth and dust
Than to endure, as Jael shall live on,
In self-contempt more bitter than the grave.
Live on and pine in long remorseful years.
Terrible tears are sequel to this deed;
Beat on thy breast, have ashes in thy hair,
Still shalt thou bear about in all thy dreams
One image, one reproach, one face, one fear.
Live, Jael, live. We shall be well revenged.

This woman was a mother, think of that;
A name which carries mercy in its sound,
A pitiful meek title one can trust;
She gave her babe the breast like other wives,
In cradle laid it, had her mother heed
To give it suck and sleep. You would suppose
She might learn pity in its helpless face;
A man asleep is weaker than a child,
And towards the weak God turns a woman's heart;
Hers being none. She is ambitious, hard,
Vain, would become heroic; to nurse babes
And sit at home, why any common girl
Is good enough for that. She must have fame;
She shall be made a song of in the camp,
And have her name upon the soldier's lip
Familiar as an oath. And when she dies
She must write Jael on the years to come;
Oblivion only terrifies her heart,
And infamy is almost twin to fame;
But rusting unremembered in the grave

Is worst of all. Let Jael rest secure,
That, if the reprobation of all time
Fall sweetly on her ashes, hers shall be
Perpetual condemnation. Ah, vain heart,
Thou shalt not lie forgotten, till the stars
Fall black into the pathways of the brine.

Can time efface a deed so wholly vile?
She stood, the mother-snake, before her tent,
She feigned a piteous dew in her false eyes,
She made her low voice gentle as a bird's,
Her one hand beckoned to the fugitive,
Her other felt along the poniard's edge
Hid near the breast where late her baby fed.
She drew the noble weary captain in ;
Her guest beneath the shelter of her home,
He laid him down to rest and had no fear.
The sacred old alliance with her clan,
The trustful calm immunity of sleep,
Sealing security each more secure.

Ah, surely, he was safe if anywhere
Beneath the mantle which she laid on him.
He was too noble to mistrust her much
His fading sense felt her insidious arm
Folding him warmly. Then he slept—she rose,
Slid like a snake across the tent—struck twice—
And stung him dead.

                God saw her, up in Heaven.
The lark outside went on with his old song.
The sheep grazed, and the floating clouds came past—
Yet it was done. Sleep, guest-right, given word,
All broken, each forgotten. She had lied
Against these holiest three and slain him there.
Bonds were as straw ; if once she thought of them,
They only gave new keenness to the nail,
And made her right hand surer for the blow.
Pah ! she will come to slay her children next
For glory and a little puff of fame ;
And so they crowned her, but her myrtle roots
In strange red soil were nurtured, and their leaves

Are never wet with rain, but fed on tears.

Then Israel came with many cymbal-girls
And clashed this noble triumph into odes,
Great pæans full of noise and shaken spears,
Loud horns and blare of battle, dust, and blood.
Then shrilled that old lean shrewing prophetess,
Grey as a she-wolf on some weaned lamb's track,
Her song of death and insult on the slain ;
Then Israel's captain holding by her skirt,
Sang second to her raving with loud words
And hare-like eyes that looked on either side,
As if in dread dead Sisera should rise
And drive him howling up the vale in fear
With nimble heels. This captain who declared
To this old scolding woman Deborah,
" Except thou goest with me I remain.
I dare not face great Sisera alone,
Unless some female fury hound me on."
The brave words of a captain brave as they,

A leader chiefly bold against the slain,
Fit jackal to the tigress which I seem,
Worthy to share the triumph of her deed,
That makes her almost viler than himself,
The craven hound tied to an old wife's strings.

My marvel is by what insidious steps
The will to slay him ripened in my mood.
For on that morning I had risen at peace,
And all my soul was calmer than a pool
Folded in vapour when the winds are gone.
Wholly at peace, I watched the ray new-born
In blessed streaks and rapid amber lanes
Run out among our vale-heads, low in heaven
One great star floated rolling yellow light.
For all night long my baby would not rest,
Till the dawn drifted, at whose coming sleep
Drew down his eyelids to my slumber song.
He could doze cradled now beyond my arms;
And, as the day was instant everywhere,

I came and made my station at the door
To draw the glory in and make it mine.
When suddenly a kind of weary mood
At all my mother life and household days
Clouded my soul and held her from delight.
It seemed such petty work, such wretched toil,
To tend a child and serve a husband's whims;
Meek, if my lord return with sullen eyes,
Glad, if his heart rejoice ; to watch his ways,
Live in his eye, hoard his least careless smile ;
Chatter with other wives, manage and hoard,
Quarrel and make it up—and then the grave,
Like fifty thousand other nameless girls,
Who took their little scrap of love and sun
Contentedly and died. Was I as these?
My dream was glory and their aim delight;
Should I be herded with their nameless dust?
Achievement seemed so easy to my hand
In that great morning. All my heart ran fire,
And turning I beheld my cradled child,

And caught the coming footstep of my lord
Crisp in the grass.   My waking life resumed
Its fetter as he came.   Content thee, drudge,
Here is thy lot ; fool not thy heart on dreams.
Then with a little weary sigh I rose
To welcome him ; and hastily put by
The vision of the morning.   As a girl,
Draping herself in secret with fine webs,
Starts at a sudden step and flings them down.
Restless he entered, gloomy, ill at ease,
Then shook himself and laughed his humour off
With an ill grace, relapsing to a frown.
And pushed about the tent arranging robes,
Searching old chests long undisturbed in dust ;
Then glancing at the wonder in my face,
Carelessly glancing, roughly he began,—
" You help me none, but marvel with big eyes
At one in household lumber elbow-deep ;
Hiding is better than the surest key.
A fight there will be ; ay, a game of blows,

Arrows and wounded men and broken wheels,—
No further than a rook flies out to feed
From this tent door. An hour remains to hide
The ore of our possessions, let the dross
Remain and sate the spearman if he comes."
" A battle," my lips faltered; all my soul
Flushed out into my face on hearing it.
Was my dream come at last? He made reply,
Misreading my emotion, " Do not fear ;
We will stand by and let them fight it out.
We have some friends at court in either camp ;
Neither will harm us, let the strong prevail.
We can await the issue and declare
For him who wins !" He laughed, and I was dumb
With bitter scorn against him in my soul,
Loathing my husband. But I tried him more—
" O lord," I said, " let me arise and arm thee.
The cause of Israel is the holy one.
These heathen are as dust upon the earth.
Let us strike in for Israel, tho' we die !"

"Ay, dame," he muttered, "he is right who wins,
And Israel may be right for all I care;
Yet Sisera is strong, and wise ones hide
When arrow sings to arrow in the air.
If right is weak, why then the God of right
Ought to be strong enough to help his own,
Without molesting one more quiet man.
But, while we chatter on, the morning ebbs,
I shall sweep off our treasure to the hills.
You and the babe may follow, as you please.
Safe is the upland, perilous the plain;
How say you?" But in scorn I turned away,
And cried, "Begone, O feeble heart." He went
Laughing and left me.
                    Then the battle shocks
Deepened all morning in the vales, and died
And freshened; but at even I beheld
A goodly man and footsore, whom I knew;
And then my dream rushed on my soul once more;
Saying, this man is weary, 'tice him in,

And slay him; and behold eternal fame
Shall blare thy name up to the stars of God.
I called him and he came.   The rest is blood,
And doom and desolation till I die!

A SKETCH AT EVENING.

The whip cracks on the plough-team's flank,
    The thresher's flail beats duller.
The round of day has warmed a bank
    Of cloud to primrose colour.

The dairy-girls cry home the kine,
    The kine in answer lowing;
And rough-haired louts with sleepy shouts
    Keep crows whence seed is growing.

The creaking wain, brushed thro' the lane,
    Hangs straws on hedges narrow;
And smoothly cleaves the soughing plough,
    And harsher grinds the harrow.

Comes, from the road-side inn caught up,
　A brawl of crowded laughter,
Thro' falling brooks and cawing rooks
　And a fiddle scrambling after.

NEMESIS.

Who may rebuke a monarch bent on wrong?
If he be rough and resolute and strong,
And tyrant of the time and fenced with master sway;
If, like a god, to him belong
The Hours to bring him sweetness on his way,
The meek Hours at his will and footstool chained all day;
To waft a little perfume of keen song
To make their lord his joy;
To smooth his brow from fold, and light
The brooding royal eyes an instant with delight;
A king who may forbid?

The man-god in his glory, crowned and calm,
Rises to reach his arm in purple hid
Towards his desire;
While in his face a hunger beams like fire;
His eyes are fate, his lips severe as death,
So that men hold their breath,
As like a whirl-wind on his wish he goes.
Who shall confront him in his deed? And say,
" Lord, thou hast wrought a shameful thing to-day;
The curse of whose misdoing may descend
To vex thy ungrown race;
Because thine iron vengeance would not bend
Or give to mercy place.
Thy lips have curled against the widow's cry,
Have sneered in some dead adversary's face;
Tyrant, assuage thy fury and amend!"
Will he not frown reply?—
" Lover of death and greedy of thy fate,
Prate not of woes to me.
Worse curses on thine intercession wait,

Thine instant, mine shall be
Hereafter ages hence, when earth is grey.
This one worm at my feet,
Let him writhe on and wither into clay;
His agony is sweet.
I will not stay my hand for any fears,
The old gods slumber long;
They are grown childish with their weight of years,
They are blind and love the strong."
Therefore are all men mute;
He rules and will not care.
No plagues of heaven refute his impious boasting there;
He reigns, and honour clothes his years supremely fair.
So of his crime he sucks the sweet, and dies
With the full savour of it in his mouth,
And keen delightful eyes.
While yet his lips a cunning laughter keep
At fools who fear the gods. So turns he to his sleep.
And all the simple people muse and say,
" His crime is surely done, and clean and passed away.

NEMESIS.

Can god account with these dry bones for wrong,
Or make them live again?
His vengeance is not wakeful, and this one
Hath made his rest, and done
His full of pleasure, and escaped god's pain."
Not so, ye fools and vain;
Heap up his grave and listen: from the ground,
From the grey bones, when years have greened his mound,
Within its circuit of sepulchral stones,
An Atè vengeance rises; soft as rain
Her footprint on the plain,
And like the fluttered leaf her lucid robe.
Wan as a dream she goes,
A floating shadow grey,
Pale-eyed, without repose,
Patient to bide the coming of her day;
Nursing her ire, till time across her path,
Fling down the helpless thing, that she may slay
The bleeding lamb delivered to her wrath.

Years are to her the shadows of one night,
Such certainty of her revenge she hath;
That, tho' they roll and roll again
And ruin all things fair,
Blood only can erase the enduring stain;
For which she watches one accursed race:
The seed of him, who ruled,
And prospered his disgrace,
Who made his laughter at the gods befooled;
And ended full of days,
Sleek and secure of fate;
Above whose resting-place
Her phantom outlines wait.
She knows, that vengeance waxes good
For keeping, as old wines;
And, tho' her veins are fire,
And all her being pines
In pain, in pain,
For the good great hunger of blood,
And the scent of the fresh sweet slain;

Yet pale in her wild want she curbs desire;
The sluggard years are slow;
Days long, hours infinite,
She bides her time to strike the blow—
And surely at last, as a flash in the night,
The signals of Nemesis sound;
At a leap, at a bound, red her hand is, and bright
Is the gash of her wound.

 Strange is the vengeance of our lords on high,
Who harm the child and pass the guilty sire;
Give him fat lands and let him calmly die
Full of sweet bread and lord of all desire.
And men look sadly as they close his eyes,
And wind him round in purple for his rest;
And, save a little murmur in the land,
They say he sleeps with the eternal blest.
Ay me, for that man's children; and again
A triple wail for those who call him sire;
Cry for the old hereditary stain,

Bemoan the Atè that can never tire.
Hope not, thou blameless son, she will refrain;
Sprinkle with ash thy head and thine attire:
Thou shalt not turn her steps, nor mitigate her ire.

RURAL EVENING.

When frogs pipe out in dripping dykes,
    And autumn wolds are sallow;
When pigeons leave the stubble spikes,
    And homeward oxen bellow.

Then, as the dun air dims the blue,
    The ditcher and his fellow
Come drenched knee-deep in pasture dew,
    And foot-clogged from the fallow :

The black frost in the white frost's wake
    Drops apples ere they mellow.
The pale sun dies behind the brake,
    The vapour rises yellow.

A lass against the mill-pool gate,
    Where dips the latest swallow,
Has set her basket down to wait
    Some sheepish country fellow.

Her rosy cheek is ripe to kiss,
    But ours are lank and hollow;
Her sun is high, ours low as this
    That ebbs o'er glooming fallow.

Our life as this fair day departs;
    Our rusty bones will follow,
Where hoary heads and weary hearts
    Rest on a churchyard pillow.

With her the wine of youth is bright,
    Death's potion we must swallow.
Time tires the soaring eagle's flight,
    Time plumes the nestling callow.

And some a wind-bound course must keep
   In shoal and glassy shallow;
While one must sail the central deep
   Where turmoil tears the billow.

One wooes in calm the vocal nine,
   One lives a genial fellow;
One bristles like a porcupine
   Or prickly rock-set aloe.

The glory of the garden rose
   Exceeds the wayside mallow.
The swan arrayed in pearly snows
   Outvies the russet swallow.

Who can predict each mortal's goal,
   A throne-step or a gallow?
But we will save a merry soul,
   And leave our judgment fallow.

RURAL EVENING.

Age shall not sour us into sneers,—
    As yields a wave-washed willow,
We to his weight of tidal years
    Will bend our branches sallow.

When ways are dim and daylight spent,
    When cold wind whistles hollow,
Come, where bright faces and content
    My ingle-corner hallow.

There logs increase the heat, old friend,
    There ale runs amber-yellow.
A waning light is ours to spend,
    A guttered end of tallow.

Come, link in mine thy hand and drink,
    And let this sentence follow,—
That sweeter tastes the bowl, whose brink
    The lips of friendship mellow.

ONE VIEW OF WORSHIP.

Seven times a day in groanings manifold,
I bend with one petition as thy slave,
My great prayer leaving lesser wants untold;
Thrice in each night I kneel out in the cold.

To this one apple in the grove of prayer
My thought, my life, my pulses turn and crave.
Earth doth not yield another boon so fair,
Hope of my youth, dream of my silver hair!

All other gifts are barren as the sea.
My field of time will only ripen weeds,
If this fruit perish unenjoyed by me.
Hearken, because I cry continually!

Men ask such vain and empty things at best,
Health, children, coin, a fair wife, merry deeds;
While these with many paltry needs molest,
Single and easy is my sole request.

Men kneel and mutter over forms by rote,
They are content with any gabbled word;
But I, with broken voice and burning throat,
On one distinct entreaty dwell and gloat.

My seething thought inclines to one desire;
A want that vexes as a grinding sword
Marrow and bone; whose abstinence to fire
Changes the common air which I respire.

Are fervid lips and idle ones the same,
Is it as one to pray or hold our peace?
If one neglect confound my words of flame
With their chill drivel, will no heart exclaim,—

"Let worship die; entreat not Zeus again
  Hard in his crust of apathetic ease;
  Control thy tears, thy bleeding heart refrain,
  He never solaced any in their pain.

"Curl up no more vain incense to his skies;
  Beat not thy breast, and eat thy bread in peace.
  Rend not thy robe, since he alone is wise
  Who sips the cup of pleasure till he dies.

"God's equal dealing differs from thine own;
  His justice is not weighed in human scale.
  He hardly hears thee bless, or heeds thee moan
  Thy hoard of curses climbing to his throne.

"Why wilt thou weary him? Thy voice ascends
  Weak, yet persistent; as an insect's wail,
  It trickles up for ever, and offends
  Where daylight into god-light rushing blends.

ONE VIEW OF WORSHIP.

"It beats the porches of eternal beams,
  Importunate it will not be denied;
  A weary echo in a land of dreams,
  Marring the tender chime of sleepy streams.

"It will not fail or be denied or sleep,
  Or cease or gather silence; as a tide
  That breaks, recurs, and breaks along the deep;
  Until a dreamer on the shore could weep,—

"So irksome is its iteration grown,—
  To get the sound away and have his rest.
  So may at length one prayer win access, thrown
  Against heaven's gate as feeble foam is blown!"

So men will change thy glory into worse,
  And idle lips will censure thee, most blest.
  I ask no miracle; that thou reverse
  The seasons, or descend in some great curse.

ONE VIEW OF WORSHIP. 145

Nature is stronger than thou art divine;
I pray not foolish for her overthrow;
That snow-time hang ripe clusters on my vine,
That rain refresh my field and only mine.

I ask not, that in spheres of ether grey
The blackened stars be torn and hurled below;
That the round sun ride eastward on his way,
That Luna draw the deeps three times a day.

But all my being withers in the want
Of one ripe, excellent, and righteous thing,
For which the sources of my nature pant
And dwell in bitter thirst until thou grant.

Wilt thou endure, while changeful seasons roll,
To watch my changeless hunger riveting
Its earnest eyes on one eternal goal?
O lord, I ask thee to complete my soul!

Count over, king, my multitude of prayers,
Number them all, if number's feeble wing
Can rise to comprehend that host of theirs ;
Which holds thee, god, my debtor unawares,

For praises unreturned, unheeded vows,
Cries in the night which had no answering,
For many moanings and unnumbered woes—
Hear, for a man gives payment where he owes.

Ah, deal not falsely, as a merchant may,
Who taketh merchandise and doth not bring
Coin to reward its use for many a day--
Nay, thou wilt hear and, *if thou canst,* repay !

A MEETING AND ADVICE.

True heart, under grey-green arches
Where the crimson cones of larches
    Bud in bristle leaves ;
Print thy feet in dewy places,
Where, amid the king-cup faces,
    The mead-spider weaves.

On the down thy raiment glistens,
In his nest the wheatear listens,
    From thee flows a lay ;
Doves refrain to pipe their trouble,
Ledges of hill fountains bubble ;
    Give thee, love, good day.

Art thou cold, because I follow
Up the wood-way, in whose hollow
    Bluebells haunt the rills?
Wind-flowers carpet all the cover,
And there come, now March is over,
    Shoaling daffodils.

Ah, my love, thy shadow only
Warms the folded dew-drop, lonely
    In secluded dells.
Hear my April prayer unchidden,
One which birds in nest-down hidden
    To their consorts tell.

Young and lonely hold no measure,
Youth's a mint of sterling treasure;
    If we hoard, we lose.
Age a coin, which Love refusing,
Out of date and out of using,
    Takes not as his dues.

A MEETING AND ADVICE.

Rose-buds, in a land of roses,
Wither ere they come to posies;
    Maiden roses mourn.
Sweet mouths many are not tasted,
Or their kisses won are wasted,
    Hour and year forsworn.

Though all ends in loveless sleep,
When the ripe hour beckons, reap—
    Reap, nor sourly say,—
" Fresh cheeks wear not weeping-stain;
Love is spoil and wedded pain
    Taint their rose away.

" Wisest he who can despise
Cupid's evanescent dyes,
    Passion's brittle prime;
He shall revel long and well
In a careless citadel,
    Monarch of his time."

A MEETING AND ADVICE.

Answer, Dove, "tho' Love's best sweet,
Like an angel's glorious feet,
    Flash and pass no more."
Answer, sweet, " Love may not last,
Yet the perfume of his past
    Lives in riper store.

" He, who wavered long at noon,
Sits alone in darkness soon,
    White with dusty snow.
Eyes can answer, hands as well,
Rusting years unlearn their spell."
    Answer, dearest, so—.

Fortune plays not twice the giver,
Leave it once and lose it ever,
    As we speak, 'tis flown.
Bind Love, ere the child-god spread
Gauzy wings above his head,
    And fickle leave his throne.

So that when thy merry weather,
Loses heart and changes feather,
  And Time's hearth is grey;
Love will save one fervid ember,
That wild east or bleak December
  Will not quench away.

THE TWO OLD KINGS.

A SKETCH AFTER KAULBACH.

ONCE two ancient kings and comrades, princes of a kindred line,
Held high wassail until midnight in a castle on the Rhine.

There around them sate their vassals, peers and pages, knights and squires;
There they long replenished beakers in the glare of pine-wood fires.

As they feasted they remembered deeds and faces turned to dust,
Days, that as sepulchral armour long had lain besmeared with rust.

In that hall forgotten faces rose above each feasting
   guest,
Dim hands trailing phantom garments, dim eyes long
   consigned to rest;
And one royal toper rising to his cousin reached the
   cup,
And the other pledged his brother as he drank the
   Rhenish up.

In his sluggish veins the vintage glowed as fire and
   nobly ran;
Till his trembling hands grew stronger, and new
   courage flushed the man,
Then he spake—" O brother, brother, we are met indeed at last
In this grey old keep, where-under roars the Rhine and
   howls the blast;
Sixty years of rolling water this great river of our land
Hath returned to father Ocean since I held thy kindred
   hand.

THE TWO OLD KINGS.

We were each then boyish princes; time ran merry; life was gold,
And our fathers held the sceptres that our sons shall shortly hold;

Beardless boys, clear-lipped as maidens then, now see this hoary fell,
Whiter than the seven mountains, fleeces down for half an ell;

Flowing over throat and breast-plate, as a broken streamlet full
Freezes over some rock's shoulder in a triple icicle.

Cousin, thou art clothed with winter underneath thy golden crown.
Many lines of many sorrows seam thy temple, track thy frown.

Old dear face with heavy eyebrows brooding o'er its buried joy;
As I search its saddened outlines hardly can I trace the boy;

As I left him in his April, as I find him in his fall,
Here where ice-bound heights are frozen in a rolling vapour's pall.

Care—we care not; nature ripens, nature renders back to clay;
Shall we, weighed with eighty winters, whine ignobly for delay?

Rather chide the tardy summons, heroes harnessed for the gloom;
Shall we linger, soured faces, carping at a grandson's bloom,

Envious of his heyday prowess?—We have memories full as fair,
We were young and we will tell it, gloating in a half despair.

Smiling at the vanished fancies, tho' our eyes are almost wet;
Scorning at the withered rosebuds, tho' we love their perfume yet.

In the dry rose of remembrance yet one petal is not
    grey;
May the month was, woods were greening, birds were
    choral, meadows gay.

On the labyrinthine pine-woods rosy clots of dawn
    rode high;
There were hunters in the forest, on that morning,
    you and I;

Then no hart, gigantic quarry, lured us thro' the
    echoing green,—
I believe, since God made woman, bluer eyes have
    never been

Than her own, my pretty wood-dove's; as we found
    her singing there,
On her brow unrisen morning, pearls of night among
    her hair.

O my love, my perished beauty, tender lamb of moun-
    tain fold;   [gold;
Little brow too wild and humble to sustain the queenly

How they rent me from thy bosom; when my royal father found,

That thy kisses were my empire; and all glory empty sound

To the joy of being near thee; thy least sigh was worth a throne;—

' Take, O sire, this hateful glory, so thou leave me to mine own;

Let my brother have mine heirship—' But they tore me from thy mouth,

Linked me to a frigid princess from the olives of the south.

We were wed; she bare me children; side by side in time to come,

Crowned we sate and clothed in purple up above the people's hum.

When I rode to fight she kissed me coldly; and, when I returned, [earned

Gave me duteous salutation as a wife should, greeting

By the victory I brought her. So we lived, and so
  she died.
She was not my love, ah, never; tho' she slumbered at
  my side.
At my side in every pageant moving with a stately
  mien;
Me she never loved, but only much she loved to be
  my queen.

Ah, my wood-girl, doth the rain beat rudely on thy
  cloister grave
In the little Saxon village? Doth the night as wildly
  rave,
As up here, with drops of tempest, rushing mist, and
  sailing cloud?—
Thro' the turmoil, lo, it rises one sweet still face in a
  shroud—

Comrade, pledge to my beloved; drink, my brother
  in renown,   [ments down.
Drink and dash the crystal beaker in a thousand frag-

THE TWO OLD KINGS.

Hail! sweet ashes—it is spoken—on to me the goblet
pass;
All is said—the cup lies broken—no vile lips shall
touch this glass."
As he ceased his cousin o'er him reached a cheering
arm and spoke,
Pointing thro' the oriel casement at the dawning where
it broke;
" Love is well, O royal brother; nothing is more sweet
in grace,
Than the tear-drop which an old man sheds upon
dead memory's face.
Love is well, regret is lovely; but and if our day is
done,
See, there rises ampler promise to new men with yonder
sun.
When our years that ripened roses only send sepulchral
weeds, [deeds?
Shall we find no consolation thinking on our famous

Strike a sterner chord, to music heroes let us march along;
Let us to the grave go pacing with a sturdier battle song.

Drink we to our dead dear comrades, loyal men, of iron might;
Who with us in front of onset felt the ecstasy of fight

Brace their sinews; for the sweetest love that ever yet was won,
Pales beside this, as a taper wan before the regal sun.

Drink we to our high ambition; drink the triumph of our throne!"
But the other aged monarch answered in an altered tone.

" Five fair kingdoms left my father; two the conquest of his spear;
I have seen their vines uprooted and their cities, red with fear,

THE TWO OLD KINGS.

Lurid heaps of smoke and cinders. I have heard the orphan's wail;
I have seen the giant Famine sitting roofless in the hail.

Of my father's laurel chaplet I have let two bay leaves fall,
I have lost two realms, whose banners flout me in my vacant hall.

And the three remaining kingdoms seem to scorn my feeble sway;
And I hear a palace murmur, that they count my life delay.

Here my huge sons stand and whisper, 'Surely he has reigned too long;
There his armour hangs rust-eaten, there his bugle, mute from song,

Never more shall waken echoes. Surely he has ruled enough;
Mark the leather of his gauntlet, how the worms are in the stuff;

How the moths have marred his mantle! There his empty baldric lies.
Shall we longer make obeisance to an old thing we despise?'
Wistful each one nods and gazes, as along the downward gloom
I descend with feeble paces to the children of the tomb."
"Nay, my brother," spoke the other, "these things are an old man's due;
Faces come and faces perish and old races cede to new.
Comrade, cheer; tho' disappointment every year remaining brings,
Shall we die faint-hearted soldiers, shall we pass despised kings?
Friends may fail and Love forsake us, Hope may falter, Faith decay,
And our pleasant dreams may open wings whereon to flee away.

Wine can stir the languid pulses to the ripeness of their youth,
Flashing back an old man's mistress in her radiance, in her truth;

Wine can make us half immortal:—nay, the years are out of tune,
Since the whispering meadows heard us whispering in the ancient June.

Let them go: we pass to silence, and our deeds are dream and nought—
Nought? Yet dreams whose recollection holds us heroes, heart and thought;

Hark, our veterans there below us talk the same refrain as we,
Harping on a faded love-song every soul in his degree;

Draining out an old experience, how an angel's golden wand
Struck the rock, and found the waters at the thirsty soul's command.

Then how purely came the torrent, till the devil changed the draught;
And the drinker rose up poisoned, with a wordling's iron craft.

How the broken years of passion cast him into sterner mould,
How the icy frost of fashion turned each genial impulse cold;

King and peer and mailèd captain, equal manhood, diverse grade,
All imperfect, hardly trembling on the skirts of lengthened shade;

Bound together, king and soldier, onwards to the land unseen,
Where the ancient heroes slumber with grey faces, cold and keen.

And, tho' we shall part to-morrow, ne'er on earth to meet again,   [Southern plain—
I beyond the Northern mountains, thou along the

See ! that morrow of our parting breaks upon our wassail feast,
Flooding on the wreathen archways early splendour from the East—

Yet still drink we our next meeting, drink it deep in beakers seven,
Brother, ended is our banquet, we will hold the next in heaven !"

ARROW OF LOVE.

Arrow of Love, is thy wound small,
Or can it slay men after all?
Dart of Desire, is thy hurt brief,
Or does its pain crown human grief?
O lip of Eros, is your breath
Gentle as sleep or harsh as death?
Ah, Love, but why in after years
Must thy son bring us burning tears?
A scar recalls thy touches bland,
Their pressure deepens to a brand.
And he, the deity of pain,
Sits pining, as a moon in wane.

His eyes are faded with despair,
The violet sickens in his hair.
And lonely in a land of reeds
He weeps his vanished days and deeds.
For ashes stain the gracious head;
The garment of his glory dead
Is rent with sighing " well-a-day !"
His wings are dusty, flakes of clay
Harden upon his comely feet;
His voice is shaken and unsweet,
Hollow and thin his answer, low
As some lamb's bleating in the snow.

Against a spit of tawny land
Love sits lamenting. On each hand
The water of a tarn is still ;
The dead clouds hang without a will.
One solitary rose-bush near,
With cankered bloom and leaves gone sere,
Is in his sight, and moves his breath

To sing about this rose's death;
And, as his thoughts are rough and few,
They make his measures rugged too.
One only cadence hears his grief,
The dry fall of each broken leaf.

The Lament.

O my fresh rose, my rose of dew,
Thy heart is stained and old;
Thy petals are no longer new,
No incense fills each purple fold.
At thy best who held thee dearer?
But June is gone and snows are nearer.

O my rose, my rose of June,
Faded daughter of the field,
Save thy perfume for a noon
Longer, and endure to yield
A little more delight, ere I am lonely
Over my dead rose, who loved one rose only.

The Answer.

O my love, my queen of May,
    The light of youth is gone.
Thy pretty tresses gather grey,
    Thy rosy lips are wan.
Will thy grey eyes alter yet,
And their nuptial smile forget?

O my love, will Time deceive,
    Will he alter true Love so?
There is more in Love, believe,
    Than the silly nations know;
More in Love when bloom is dead
Than the roses round his head.

O my love, and if thou need
    Harbour when the north-winds blow;
If thy tender foot-prints bleed
    On the flints among the snow;
Love will raise a sheltered cot,
Where the ice-blast enters not.

O my true-love, we are wise;
    When snow whitens all our land,
Underneath the cloudy skies
    We will travel hand in hand.
Since we have not far to go
To our rest beyond the snow.

Conclusion.

So Love lamented by the brim,
And I arose and answered him.
Until his rainy eyes became
Divine once more with subtle flame.
And down he leant to glean again
His arrows scattered on the plain;
And hitched his shoulder-quiver right,
And felt his loosened bow-string tight;
And shook the tresses from his eyes,
And gave a few short dreamy sighs;
Until a sunbeam smote his wing;
He shivered lightly at its sting;

ARROW OF LOVE.

And with a slow smile then arose,
But in departure one fair rose
Fell from his crown; and so he past;
While o'er the sullen mere-waves fast
Beams numberless in golden beads
Rocked on the ripples and the reeds.

ODE TO THE SUN.

With sound thy car ascends from ocean soundless,
    In horns of light;
Beyond, around, beams enter into boundless
    Grey halls of night.

Thy wheels roll over regions thunder-wasted,
    Blue fields divine
On giant mountain clouds, whence none have tasted
    The berry of wine.

The ray-gloss on thy wings is amber, shaken
    To rosy showers;
Thy voice is on the waters, and they waken
    Like a field of flowers.

ODE TO THE SUN.

Thy word is as a lyre-beat or the laughter
    Of loves unseen;
Thy gleam as one sweet tear that gathers after,
    When joys grow keen.

Thou sayest, I have no lot or hand in slumber;
    I am Light, supreme.
My robes of glory quench the planet number,
    As Day pales Dream.

The soft Moon is my sister and my shadow;
    Her torch is mild,
Among the globe-flowers of my heavenly meadow
    She moves a child.

She has stolen a drop of incense at mine altar,—
    Some light I leave
To make Heaven fair around her, when I falter
    In lines of eve.

She is given a little reign between my splendours;
    Her intervals
Sustain with rest each soul, who homage renders
    At festivals

Of me, great Phœbus, pinnacled in ardours;
    Whose tyrant throne
Burns in blown cloud behind the ocean harbours,
    As ruby stone.

In the dimness of my regent anguish strengthens
    The sick man's sighs;
The miser shudders as the shadow lengthens,
    The raven cries.

The sap of leaves, the blood in birds, of fishes,
    The world's pulse, wane.
The doors of sense are barred with sleepy wishes
    And phantom pain.

Till in the garden of the grave the nations
    Discern my beam;
And rise up heartened with my consolations
    From nets of dream.

I refresh all things, save the blind dead faces
    With lips at peace.
These dead are mighty in their charnel places,
    I cheer not these.

Their lips are unrefreshed with drops of thunder;
    Their eyelids worn
Are never lifted to my way in wonder
    At eve or morn.

But bitter dust is in their teeth to swallow;
    Their heart is stone;
What Lord is he whom these blind dreamers follow?
    I know not one!

But dim dry roots shall bud; on fallows poorest
    Sour bents shall shine;
And wasted wrinkled heights be clothed with forest;—
    These are my sign!

In grass-land shall arise a sound of heifers,
    A voice of herds;
I bathe my glowing hands in breathing zephyrs,
    I call the birds.

In ripple and perfume and deep breezy lustre
    My flame-feet tread;
My girdle sprinkles moons in many a cluster,
    As sand is shed;

Prodigal beams, and flakes, and ardent arrows
    Are my Light's tide;
A mighty flood, whose channel never narrows
    Or waves subside.

ODE TO THE SUN.

I am the gates of life. My dawn is burning
    With foam of stars,
Bright as the margin of a wave returning
    In refluent bars.

The rain wails not around my palace chamber;
    There day-long glows
Increase and deepen from Auroral amber
    To Vesper's rose.

The planets veil their burning faces near me;
    The green world's ends
Flash up through miles of ether that uprear me;
    Pale vapour blends

In underneath, unfolds itself or closes,
    Divides, dilates;
The Sea, my path-way, spreads her deep with roses
    To my red gates.

When Ocean's rocking floors are wrought with anger,
    When sore the sea;
The heart of Earth is heavy in her danger,
    Her cry for me.

She rears her regal head, as my orb passes,
    With weary eyes;
Her long hands fruitful thro' the roots and grasses
    Yearn at my skies.

"In travail of great seas I faint surrounded,"
    She wails distressed;
"Too long have billows beaten in and wounded
    My patient breast.

"Too long the wasteful waves eat out mine islands,
    Pluck at my sides,
Draw down my sea-board cities into silence
    With barren tides.

"With rain and rush of breakers hath contended
    My hollow form;
Am I, God's daughter, to endure unfriended
    The lash of storm?

"Ray out and quench, the furious deep will hear thee;
    Ah, lord, descend!
Curb those wild horses of the foam; they fear thee;
    Their riot end!"

Earth cries; her eyes are dim with sand; her mournful
    Dumb hands bewail,
Naked, in mute appeal against the scornful
    And haggard hail.

Till I unfold my glory as a mantle;
    Till my red arm
Lull down the chidden breakers into gentle
    Ripples of calm.

Then Earth curls up her incense to my palace;
    Her fanes are full.
The Flamen rolls libations, and his chalice
    Is crowned with wool.

The rows of altar-girls with ringing voices,
    And youths with lyres,
Sing to the radiant father, who rejoices
    To hear their choirs.

The wafted echo of their measure answers
    To the sun-steeds' hooves;
The rhythmic limbs and raiment of the dancers
    Flash in far groves.

What words are these, that, rolled around me driving,
    Proclaim me blest?
Sweet as the wrestle of my reins arriving
    In fields of rest,—

"All hail, eternal Phœbus, king of ether,
    Ruler of rays;
Storm and the deep thou bindest in thy tether,
    God of Heaven's ways!"

A MADRIGAL.

LOVE GIVES ALL AWAY.

"And what is Love by nature?"
   My pretty true-love sighs.
And I reply, in feature
   A child with pensive eyes,

An infant forehead shaded
   With many ringlet rings,
And pearly shoulders faded
   In the colour of his wings.

His ways are those of children
   Who come to be caressed;
Or, as a little wild wren
   Who fears to leave her nest,—

A MADRIGAL.

He is shy; if one shall beckon;
    He hides, will not obey;
He spends, and will not reckon,
    For Love gives all away.

He hoards to lavish only,
    And lives in miser way.
Now hermit-like is lonely,
    Now gallant-like is gay.

Slay Love, he is not broken;
    Wound him, his hurt will heal.
More than his lips have spoken
    His cunning eyes reveal.

His sighs the still air sweet'n,
    As primrose woods do May.
His locks are pale, as wheaten
    Fields in the wan moon-ray.

His palm is always tender;
   His eyes are rainy grey.
His wage-return is slender;
   For Love gives all away.

His aspect, as he muses,
   Is paler than the dead;
He weeps more when he loses,
   Than he laughs when he is fed.

Love at a touch will falter,
   Love at a nod will stay;
But armies cannot alter
   One hair-breadth of his way.

He trembles at a rose-leaf,
   And rushes on a spear.
A thorn-prick and he shows grief,
   But Death he cannot fear.

A MADRIGAL.

The tyrant may not quench him,
    He laughs at prison bars;
The water-floods may drench him,
    The fire may give him scars.

Though thou lay chain and fetter
    On ankle, wrist, and hands,
He will not serve thee better,
    But soar to unknown lands.

He follows shadow faces
    Into grave-yards unawares.
He reaps in sterile places,
    And brings home sheaves of tares.

One tear will heal his anger;
    He will wait and watch all day;
He scoffs at toil and danger,
    His last crust gives away.

He will strip off his raiment
   To make his dear one gay;
And will laugh at any payment,
   Having given all away.

When care his heart engages,
   And his rose-leaf gathers grey,
He will claim a kiss for wages,
   And demand a smile for pay.

THE GARDEN OF DELIGHT.

Slumber, child, sweet-heart of Eròs, and dream in thy
   lover's own garden,
Where the sweet apple abounds and the myrtles are
   many and deep;
Rest, he has watch at thy pillow of rose-petals shed
   ere they harden;
Rest, if a harsh wind arise then his wing shall be round
   thee in sleep.

If a sunbeam alight on his darling, the god will arise
   and give shadow;
If a droning importunate bee loiter, he makes it go by;

Tho' it seek to no flower that is sweeter than this
    sleeping one in its meadow;
No honey-bloom equals his own in the lands where
    the asphodels lie.

Dream, therefore, love's child-love, serenely, thy suitor
    will helm thee sweet vision;
Some shadows are baleful of night; he will heed that
    he guide them away.
He will breathe on thine eyelids a dream drawn down
    from the valeheads elysian,
Painted with rainbow and set to the music of mur-
    muring spray.

Lest thy soul pine for his in the absence of sleep, lest
    another be near thee,
He will send thee his glorified form, more a god than
    he dares be awake.

O my child, the intense very Eròs with beams of his
   presence would sear thee;
Therefore he softens his rays; his effulgence he dims
   for thy sake.

Ah, slumber is well, but the rising is better, my queen,
   as the shaken
Pictures of orchards in waves echo back the gold
   apples less clear;
So 'tis sweeter, if Eròs with burning lips over thee
   whisper, to waken;
Then arise for his doves are around and no ravens of
   Anteros near.

IN SICILY.

Yonder is Ætna purple with one cloud.
Below us the enduring water-sound
Arises, broken where the vineyard men
Sing in their houses; under and below
The long Tyrrhenian islands meet the foam;
Then the illimitable sea rolls in,
Where the lights pass; until the rosy space
Of ether deepens into olive grey;
And rays the floating purple like a hand,
Or holds the gates of light in violet waves.

Why art thou silent, voice of my desire?
Be pitiful and answer, lest I feel

This mighty dream unreal as the touch
Of thy sweet hand that lulls my soul asleep.
Bend thine eyes, beautiful with all their light,
Full on my face ; let thy lips follow them ;
Lest I should fear delusion, and awake
Hereafter weeping for a phantom joy.

What have I done to merit love of thine,
How shall I rise up worthy of mine own?
Honour enough for any lips of mine
To kiss the little broken cistus bud
Slain by thy rosy feet at some cliff edge.

Wonder of Eros, this and thus was I ;
The dull weak thing, whose instinct at thy face
Drave him to fall in adoration prone.
He saw thy beauty terrible as fire,
His feeble nature faltered as in pain.
Marvel of love, whose empire alters all,
Since thou hast deigned to raise me to thy smile ;

As the moon calls a low and earth-born cloud
To ascend and glisten in her glorious arms,
Till in his vapour all her form is lost;
But he who veils her round glows more and more.

As in a silence of warm air the lark
Sings, in thy love my spirit is content;
As in a waste of many buds the bee
Is busy with much perfume, till it tire;
I am broken with the sweetness of my love.
I feel thy spirit brooding in serene
Completeness, deep as ether, pure as dew.
The still hours come and watch us and depart.
At length, beyond the glory of a star,
Thou dost arise; and, in thy leaving me,
Soothest my burning forehead with thy hand.
Or, in caress that runs before farewell,
I watch thee gather back thy heavy curls
Disordered; leaning in a silent care
To smile, before thy lips are moved to mine;

Lest I should lose thy smile, as intense light
Is lost if men consider it too near.
So leaning drink my soul into thine own;
Have thy sweet arm about me, and begin
A murmuring breath in whisper, as the talk
Of mated swallows when their nest is laid.
My flower of dawn, my bud with timid folds,
My lily, quailing ere the light is laid
Or rain goes on thy petals; O my song
Borne brokenly as a moth in perfumed air;
My silver cloud of spices consecrated,
O incense of my altar; last, my love;
Rest in that name of all the number best!
Ah, but to rest with thy sweet serious eyes
Above my slumber; that were lovely dream,
Worthy a lord of heaven, whose stately joy
Immortally continues. Whisper me
In living silence: thy smooth cheek on mine:
And let thy ringlet flakes efface the day
With clustered ripples from my glowing eyes.
And so remain as radiant as of yore.

Mysterious in thy beauty; till this heart
Dissolve to equal thine and pulse with thine,
In larger beatings, as a god's that loves,—
Until arterial ichors change the stream
Of puny life within me.   Till I drain
Enormous inspiration at thy lips;
For surely they who love become as gods
Knowing all wisdom; and thy love shall draw
My faltering soul invested in its power,
Out and beyond this tumult we call Time.
Where the loud fruitless billows heave themselves,
Where the long heedless clouds roll and are lost—
Where one year's blossom is the next one's dust.
And summer's wife may fade to winter's dead.
The infants of her love surround her urn
Year after year with unenduring wreaths;
The dim sweet face fades from them.   Children's eyes
Weep nothing long, and she shall be forgot
Out in the lonely grasses of her rest.

  Across the silver lyre-beat of my love,
Intrudes a chord of death! a moaning wire

Changes the honied cadence at its close.
Let the song cease. Ah, me, my beautiful,
Let us be very busy with our joy,
While there is light above us and sweet air.
I question not beyond thee. Love is more
Than Time: thine eyes are on me, and thy palm
Is wound with mine: thy lucid orbs resume
Old tenderness, and wean me from the thought
Beyond thine arms: thine instant, love, is more
Than all hereafter, when the immeasurable
Cycles of darkness brood above our graves
For ever. Leave me this, that I may hear
The breathings of thy bosom, hear thy sighs
Drawn out in long suppression from thy soul,
To tell me more than language all thy love.
Leave this, I question not while this endure:
Beautiful dream, be patient and delay
A little while; and leave us hand in hand
To watch the dædal changes of the woods,
The wave, the vineyard, and the floating heads
Of Ætna, islanded in amber cloud.

THE SHEPHERD AND THE HIRELING.

A MONKISH DOGGREL.

Who keepeth his sheep in the wattled fold?
A wise man godly, merry, and old.
His own is the flock and he loves it well,
As the grey wolves under the forest can tell;
When a rough one comes he stands very fast,
With his staff and his hounds and his stones to cast,
>   For his sheep, safe sheep!

Who foldeth his sheep on the hill that is red?
A sleepy, hireling fellow instead.
His sheep are another's; he careth none
Tho' the wolves are rending them one by one.
When the grey beast comes, he fleeth away
Down the hill like a feather; ah, well-a-day
>   For his sheep, poor sheep!

Who tethers our flock in the Church her yard?
A merry good saint who is honest and hard.
His sheep know the Bishop, he knows his sheep,
So, when a lean heretic tries to creep,
He raises his crook and his gold hoop-ring
And scares him away, while the choristers sing
    For their souls, safe souls.

Who foldeth his swine in the city of sin?
The bloat brown Satan burning within.
He pushes on each to his trough with a prong
And away to perdition goads them along.
When an angel hovers, he shouts him away
And gathers them muck till the judgment day.
    Well-a-day, poor souls.

He pastures them well in a forest tall,
And beats on the boughs till the acorns fall;
In each of their snouts he rivets his ring,
And drags them in where the old nettles sting;
On each of their withers right plain to see
He brands them deep with a gothic D,
    Poor swine, poor souls!

Now sing we together for souls, and sheep
Who sit on the hills where the night lies deep.
May they gain a good grass that is sweet to feast,
And never be scared by a prowling beast.
This is my carol, God help us, Sirs,
And keep you each clean of such evil curs;

                In æternum, Amen.

AT THE COUNCIL.

I stood to-day in that great square of fountains;
    And heard the cannons of St. Angelo
In many echoes towards the Alban mountains
    Boom over Tiber's flow.

I saw the nations throng thy burnished spaces,
    Cathedral of the universe and Rome;
One purpose held those earnest upturned faces
    Under the golden dome.

Tumult of light rolled on that human ocean;
    Climax of sound replied in organ storms;
And shook those altar Titans into motion,
    Bernini's windy forms.

They seemed to toss their giant arms appealing
    Where Angelo with mighty hand has striven
To paint his angels on an earthly ceiling
    Grander than those of heaven.

Mid-air among the columns seemed to hover
    Incense in clouds above that living tide.
Whence are these come, who tread thy courts, Jehovah,
    In raiment deep and dyed?

"We are gathered thine elect among all races;
    As at God's birth with Magian kings, afar
Thy whisper found us in our desert places,
    Where we beheld thy star,

"Ninth Piety of Rome; with whom the keys are,
    Regent to hold God's house, to feed his flock
Where Cæsar ruled; and thou, supplanting Cæsar,
    Art firm on Peter's rock.

"Nicæa's thunders yet are fresh as morning
    Beams in whose light the church has gone and goes,
To-day Nicæa peals in Rome her warning;
    Pontiff to curse thy foes

"We come, Armenia, Gaul, Missouri, Britain;
    The chosen of the chosen priests are there.
To all men hath gone out his mandate written,
    Who fills St. Peter's chair.

"Grey heads have waves Atlantic wafted scathless
    Weak feet have toiled o'er Libyan hills in fear,
Old Bishops from the regions of the faithless
    Have crept on crutches here.

"To far Canadian meres of ice-bound silence,
    To cities lost in continents of sand,
To shoaling belts around Pacific islands,
    The Pontiff raised his hand.

"Then with one mind they came, the Bishop leaders,
  The outpost Captains of the Church at fight,
From uplands clothed with Lebanonian cedars,
  From realms of Arctic night;—

"Lo, we are ready at thy summons, father;
  Loose, and we loosen, bind and we will bind.
The conclave princes at thy blast shall gather
  As red leaves after wind.

"Thunder the doctrine of this last evangel,
  Clear as the note of doom its accents sound!
While men regard thine aspect, as an angel
  In the sun's orb and crowned!

"At thy reproof let nations quail in terror,
  And tremble at the pealing of thy word,
For God has made thy mouth his own, and error
  In thy voice is not heard.

"Let all be doomed on whom thy curses thunder,
   Let none be righteous whom thou dost withstand;
The priesthood of a word we kneel in wonder,
   And kiss thy sacred hand."

"Hear, shade of Calvin, ghost of Luther, hearken,
   Ye renegades of northern yesterday;
Infidel bones, which years of silence darken,
   Turn and salute our ray!

"Leave vain philosophies, old dreamer Teuton,
   Great drowsy fly in webs of logic weak;
We silenced Galileo, menaced Newton,
   And Darwin shall not speak.

"Behold a sign, ye sceptic sons of evil,
   The dogma; raising which, as Michael, brave
Our pope, confront their scientific Devil
   Over each unclosed grave;

" Till Death and Doubt be thy tame sheep, O pastor,
   Pontiff of souls and vicar of God's choice,—
Infallible ; in whom the spirit-master
   Hath breathed his spirit voice,—

" Explain our Faith !   All faithful hear thy mandate,
   Emperors watch in dread our world debate ;
Thy fear is on all peoples ! " (but the bandit,
   Who plunders at thy gate.)

Rome, November, 1869.

THE END.

PRINTED BY TAYLOR AND CO.,
LITTLE QUEEN STREET, LINCOLN'S INN FIELDS.

BY THE SAME AUTHOR.

PHILOCTETES; a Metrical Drama, after the Antique. Crown 8vo, 4s. 6d.

OPINIONS OF THE PRESS.

"This is a fine poem, beautiful in detail, powerful as a whole; leaving the same sort of impression of sad majesty upon us as many of the finest Greek dramas themselves: combining the self-restrained and subdued passion of the antique style, with here and there a touch of that luxuriance of conception, and everywhere that wider rage of emotions and deeper love of natural beauty, characteristic of the modern, ... all these elements form together a poem of the noblest kind, in which a subject truly Greek is just illuminated with the dawn of that which still lay below the horizon of Sophocles. It is not that the poet assumes any thoughts absolutely invisible to the great poets of the great age of Greece, but that knowing as he does the clear and brighter faith to which these thoughts were tending, he gives them a greater emphasis and a richer glow than was possible to the great Greek poet."—THE SPECTATOR, *June 30th*, 1866.

'Philoctetes,' a drama after the antique, which took hold of all readers having any pretension to taste and scholarship on its first appearance."—CONTEMPORARY REVIEW, *October*, 1867.

"'Philoctetes,' a poem so good that many were anxious to know by whom it was written."—EXAMINER, *December 17th*, 1870.

"Equally fine are some of the choric passages in the 'Philoctetes' of the Hon. J. Leicester Warren, one of the first of our young poets."—ST. PAUL'S MAGAZINE, *September*, 1872.

In writing 'Philoctetes' the author has proved himself capable of a really admirable imitation of the Greek drama." LONDON REVIEW, *July 20th*, 1867.

"The author of 'Philoctetes' has been well known among all lovers of poetry."—WESTMINSTER REVIEW, *January*, 1871.

"There is fine poetry in 'Philoctetes,' but it is the song of despair."—READER, *May 19th*, 1866.

"The classical field is open and unrifled. Let the author pursue his researches amongst its treasures, and go on to delight his generation with fresh studies 'from the antique' as truthfully conceived as his 'Philoctetes.'"—SATURDAY REVIEW, *August 18th*, 1866.

"An unknown writer who chooses as the subject of a 'metrical drama, after the antique,' the sufferings and deliverance of Philoctetes, and so challenges comparison with all but the noblest of the extant works of Sophocles enters on a task of no common magnitude ... We may add to that plea that the enterprise, bold as it undoubtedly was, has issued not in failure but in success. The modern 'Philoctetes' will be read with pleasure by those who have loved and admired the old. It deserves to the full as high a place in the literature of our time as Mr. Arnold's 'Merope,' or Mr. Swinburne's 'Atalanta in Calydon.'"—CONTEMPORARY REVIEW, *June*, 1866.

REHEARSALS; a Book of Verses. Crown 8vo, 6s.
OPINIONS OF THE PRESS.

"The author has found his gift; and its presence is visible more or less in every piece on which he has now tried his hand. This gift we take to be a compound of rich fancy and imagination, fostered by a keen and loving insight of nature, and kept in cheque by a sustained and observant study of the antique models which, better than any later examples, supply lessons of form and chasteness to modern verse-writers. In 'Rehearsals' the impress of this may be traced throughout; on some of the poems it is so deeply and successfully set that, unless the taste for poetry is extinct, they cannot fail to survive the ephemeral notice which may be drawn to them by magazines and reviews, and to hold their own amidst those samples of the English muse of the nineteenth century which are worthy to live."—SATURDAY REVIEW, *December* 10*th*, 1870.

"Mr. Warren, whom we may be allowed to congratulate on claiming in his own person the honours which he has won under the name of 'William Lancaster,' expresses with uncommon energy and passion the spirit of 'revolt' which is so common among our young poets, we may say, among our young thinkers. ... Mr. Warren has in no small measure the gifts of the poet, but we cannot hope or even wish for him the highest success till he can come to believe in light."—SPECTATOR, *February* 4*th*, 1871.

"'Rehearsals' not merely justifies all the praises which have been bestowed upon the previous poems, but shows that Mr. Warren is capable of still greater achievements. His present volume reveals a sustained power of thought, a ripeness of judgment, and an artistic beauty, for which we were quite unprepared."—WESTMINSTER REVIEW, *January*, 1871.

"Mr. Warren has an exquisite ear; and his verse dwells on the ear of the reader with a whisper as of evening wind stealing through woodbine, always too with a shade of melancholy in its sweetness. What could be tenderer, sweeter, more rapt in self-nursed despair than this from 'The Children of the Gods?'. . . . 'Pandora' is an exquisite restoration. It is instinct with the Greek spirit. The severe simplicity and beauty of the old life speaks through the swell of the rhythm, which pulses steady and calm, like the waves of a summer sea round rocks."—NONCONFORMIST, *Dec. 14th,* 1870.

"We cannot help recognizing in 'Rehearsals' the mature work of a ripe poet. The promise of his 'Philoctetes' and 'Orestes' made us sure that, in the course of a few years, their author would produce poetry worthy to take its place amidst the more memorable out-pouring of contemporary verse-weavers."—LITERARY CHURCHMAN, *January 5th,* 1871.

"Mr. Warren has a quick eye and ear for the sights and sounds of external nature; and a warm, sympathizing heart with the most tragic as well as the most tender emotions of human nature. His genius takes many forms, and is equally well sustained in its multiform versatility. His chief poems in this collection are all written on subjects as different and as distinct in their character as can well be imagined, and yet they are all remarkable for high finish, vigour, and poetical insight. . . Of all the pieces in the volume, we give the palm of excellence to 'Expostulation,' which is a passionate appeal of the God of Israel to the people who have forsaken him. We have space to quote only a few lines of this very beautiful poem.—THE GRAPHIC, *February, 18th,* 1871.

"Mr. Warren's 'Rehearsals' consists of forty-four poems, all of them short, many terse almost to abruptness. Nevertheless, each poem is pleasant to read, for they are all carefully composed and well put together. . . . 'An Ode' is one of the finest poems in 'Rehearsals.' The following as the three closing stanzas of it. . . . A land of a rest and sleep is here so powerfully shown to be the goal for which alone it is wise to long. . . . It ('The Prodigal Son') is a poem of only three verses, but it is powerful in its simplicity and terseness. With it we may close this short review of Mr. Warren's book, but not without expressing a hope that before long he will give us more of his work, which, we have fair grounds for hoping, will fulfil the promise he has undoubtedly shown in these poems and in 'Philoctetes.'"—SCOTSMAN, *May 25th,* 1871.

"His (the author's) descriptions of nature are remarkably faithful, and there is great finish in all that he writes."—WEEKLY REVIEW, *March 25th,* 1871.

"We have already said that the music of the verse is often exceedingly charming, and without close study in several of the poems, admiration of the technical skill of the artist might induce the reader to overlook the strength of the thought so elegantly and tersely expressed."—MANCHESTER EXAMINER AND TIMES, *March 22nd*, 1871.

"There is no mistake whatever about the genius and ability of Mr. Warren. ... It is possible that the introduction which we propose to give our readers to this remarkably fine volume may as well begin with this horribly beautiful poem. (The Strange Parable) ... If Mr. Warren write a *little* slower he will leave marks behind him."—DAILY REVIEW, *December 19th*, 1870.

"So long as poems like this can be written in the nineteenth century, so long may we say that the warmth and spirit of the old classic religion did not expire with Goethe. ... The most biting sarcasm, and the tenderest feeling, the keenest sensibility to natural beauty, the utmost freedom from coarse sensuousness, the deepest inspiration and the highest aspiration, the saddest undertone and the sweetest melody, all lie between the covers of this book.—THE ILLUSTRATED REVIEW, 1870.

ORESTES; a Metrical Drama. Crown 8vo, 4s. 6d.

OPINIONS OF THE PRESS.

"In 'Orestes,' he (the author) has at least proved himself capable of producing an admirable piece of English composition. Some of the blank verse in this poem is almost Shakesperean in its forcible expression, in its power of clearly realizing the subtleties of the thought of which it is the vehicle, in its freedom from affectation, in its freedom from weakness. ... When we meet such poetry as this book contains, the temptation to quote is irresistible."—LONDON REVIEW, *July 20th*, 1867.

"The present work, like its predecessor, 'Philoctetes,' contains many passages, especially in the choruses, the force and beauty of which are not to be denied. ... Viewed merely as a dramatic poem, it often demands high praise for the force of its dialogue, and for the fervid spirit and beauty of description evinced in the choruses. There is the true throb of passion in the reproaches which Orestes addresses to his mother, whom he still believes guilty of seeking his life."—ATHENÆUM, *July 27th*, 1867.

"Altogether, this 'Orestes' is a fine conception, powerfully wrought out and calculated, unless we greatly err, to sustain its author's well-won place among the foremost imitators of the ancient drama."—CONTEMPORARY REVIEW, *October*, 1867.

STRAHAN & Co., 56, Ludgate Hill, London.

NEW BOOKS.

REVELATION CONSIDERED AS LIGHT; a a Series of Discourses. By the Right Rev. ALEXANDER EWING, D.C.L., Bishop of Argyll and the Isles. Post 8vo.

WHITE ROSE and RED. By the Author of 'Saint Abe and his Seven Wives.' Crown 8vo.

NATIONAL EDUCATION and PUBLIC ELEMENTARY SCHOOLS. By JAMES H. RIGG, D.D. Crown 8vo.

The CHARACTER of ST. PAUL. By J. S. HOWSON, D.D., Dean of Chester. Crown 8vo.

OLD MASTERS and THEIR PAINTINGS. By SARAH TYTLER, Author of 'Papers for Thoughtful Girls.' Crown 8vo.

MODERN PAINTERS and THEIR PICTURES. By SARAH TYTLER, Author of 'Papers for Thoughtful Girls.' Crown 8vo.

OULITA: a Tragedy. By the Author of 'Friends in Council.' New Edition. 18mo.

THE GAOL CRADLE — WHO ROCKS IT? Crown 8vo.

LAUTERDALE: a New Story. 3 vols. Post 8vo.

LARS: a Pastoral of Norway. By BAYARD TAYLOR. Small 8vo. 3s. 6d.

The TRAGEDIES of ÆSCHYLOS. A New Translation; with a Biographical Essay, and an Appendix of Rhymed Choral Odes. By E. H. PLUMPTRE, M.A., Professor of Divinity, King's College, London. Popular Edition. In 1 vol. crown 8vo. 7s. 6d.

STRAHAN & Co., 56, Ludgate Hill, London.

NEW BOOKS.

MEMORIALS of a QUIET LIFE. By Augustus J. C. HARE, Author of 'Walks in Rome.' With Two Steel Portraits. Seventh Edition. 2 vols. crown 8vo. 21s.

The SOUL'S LEGEND. By DORA GREENWELL. Crown 8vo. 2s.

POLITICAL PORTRAITS. Characters of some of our Public Men. Reprinted from the *Daily News*. Revised, and with Additional Sketches. Third Edition. Crown 8vo. 6s.

SOME TALK ABOUT ANIMALS and THEIR MASTERS. By the Author of 'Friends in Council.' Crown 8vo. 7s. 6d.

WALKS in FLORENCE. By SUSAN and JOANNA HORNER. With Illustrations. Second Edition. 2 vols. crown 8vo. 21s.

SEEN and HEARD. By the Author of 'Occupations of a Retired Life.' 3 vols. post 8vo. 31s. 6d.

The TRUE HISTORY of JOSHUA DAVIDSON. Fourth Edition. Crown 8vo. 5s.

HINDOO TALES; or, the Adventures of Ten Princes. Freely translated from the Sanskrit of the Dasakumaracharitam. By P. W. JACOB. Crown 8vo. 6s.

GOLDEN LIVES: Biographies for the Day. By H. A. PAGE. With Illustrations. Second Edition. Crown 8vo. cloth extra, 5s.

OUR NEW MASTERS. By THOMAS WRIGHT (the "Journeyman Engineer"). Post 8vo. 9s.

WANDERINGS in SPAIN. By AUGUSTUS J. C. HARE. With Illustrations. Third Edition. Crown 8vo. 10s. 6d.

MEN of the THIRD REPUBLIC. Reprinted, with large Additions, from the *Daily News*. Crown 8vo. 6s.

STRAHAN & Co., 56, Ludgate Hill, London.

www.ingramcontent.com/pod-product-compliance
Lightning Source LLC
Chambersburg PA
CBHW031815220426
43662CB00007B/660